SINNER'S ADVOCATE

SINNER'S ADVOCATE

AN LDS PERSPECTIVE ON THE MORALITY OF CRIMINAL DEFENSE

TAYLOR HARTLEY

BONNEVILLE BOOKS
SPRINGVILLE, UTAH

Names have been changed to protect privacy.

This is not an official publication of The Church of Jesus Christ of Latter-day Saints. The opinions and views expressed herein belong solely to the author and do not necessarily represent the opinions or views of Cedar Fort, Inc. Permission for the use of sources, graphics, and photos is also solely the responsibility of the author.

ISBN 13: 978-1-59955-799-1
Published by Bonneville Books, an imprint of Cedar Fort, Inc.,
2373 W. 700 S., Springville, UT 84663
Distributed by Cedar Fort, Inc., www.cedarfort.com

LIBRARY OF CONGRESS CATALOGING-IN-PUBLICATION DATA

Hartley, Taylor C. (Taylor Charles), 1978- author.
Sinner's advocate : an LDS perspective on the morality of criminal defense / Taylor C. Hartley, Esq.
pages cm
Summary: Discussion on how a lawyer can be a member of the Church of Jesus Christ of Latter-day Saints in good standing and also defend criminals.
ISBN 978-1-59955-799-1
1. Defense (Criminal procedure)--Moral and ethical aspects. 2. Legal ethics. 3. Criminal justice, Administration of--Moral and ethical aspects. 4. Religion and law. 5. Church of Jesus Christ of Latter-day Saints--Doctrines. I. Title.
K5455.H37 2011
174'.3--dc22

2011006541

Cover design by Danie Romrell
Cover design © 2011 by Lyle Mortimer
Edited and typeset by Melissa J. Caldwell

Printed in the United States of America
10 9 8 7 6 5 4 3 2 1
Printed on acid-free paper

To Ken Peay, Peter James Spicer, Derek Bailey, Jason Hartley, Brent Hartley, Sheldon Carter, Gary D. Stott, Dave Clark, and Craig Johnson

CONTENTS

SECTION I: The Issue and Personal History

1. *The Issue: Defending the Criminal* 3
2. *Personal History: The Heart of a Social Worker and the Mind of a Lawyer* 7
3. *The Job that Strips Away Nearly All Limits on Optimism* 15
4. *Leniency vs. Mercy* 19

SECTION II: Evidentiary Standards and Standards of Truth, Degrees of Certainty, and Spiritual Truth Scrutiny and Their Application to the Accused

5. *Evidentiary Standards* 27
6. *Evidentiary Standards and the Reality of Reason* 33
7. *Tying the Evidentiary Standards Together with the Degrees of Certainty about Spiritual Truths* 41
8. *The Law's Evidentiary Standards and Alma's Degrees of Spiritual Certainty* 49
9. *Introduction to the Tests and the Rational Basis Test* 61
10. *Intermediate Scrutiny* 77
11. *Strict Scrutiny* 81
12. *Intellectual Certainty: Knowledge by Extension and Failure to State a Claim upon Which True Religion Can Be Founded* 93

13. Personal Preferences: The Benefits of Strict Scrutiny 105

SECTION III: Applying Scrutiny to People, and Especially to the Guilty, and Becoming More Compassionate

14. Applying the Scrutiny Tests in Order to Scrutinize People 115

15. An Example of Make-Believe Concerning How to Treat the Wicked. 117

16. Make-Believe Elsewhere 119

17. Scriptural Justifications for Defending Criminals 129

18. The Real-Life Examples: Who These Criminals Really Are 167

19. Process of Elimination and Testimony 175

About the Author 183

SECTION I

THE ISSUE AND PERSONAL HISTORY

1

THE ISSUE: DEFENDING THE CRIMINAL

WHILE DRIVING HOME LATE ONE NIGHT FROM DUGWAY PROVING Grounds, a military base in the west desert of Utah, I received a call from his brother. He told me that Rico, who was a young father in his early twenties, had been charged with attempted murder. This brother was trying to find an attorney for Rico. After I was retained, I learned about the facts of the case.

One evening, Rico Martinez and his friends were at a gas station refueling their vehicle. Another vehicle approached to fill up. The new arrival was a group from an opposing gang. Rico, one of his friends, and the occupants of the newcomer's vehicle began flashing signs at one another. The opposing gang members drove past the vehicle Rico had been traveling in as a passenger and hit the hood with a bat, leaving a dent, then sped off.

About four hours later, at roughly 10:30 p.m., the rival gang members saw Rico's vehicle approaching from behind. The vehicle accelerated down the neighborhood hill, pulled to the side of the opposing gang vehicle, and drove in parallel with them in the wrong lane of traffic.

The driver looked over and saw Rico in the passenger seat. My client was reaching out of the front passenger window with his arm, shoulder, and head, holding a black handgun in his fist. The frequent street lamps and light reflecting off the snow-covered ground showed that Rico was looking at the driver with concentrated intent and pinched lips. Rico was close enough that the driver could see the shaved facial hair on his chin, his Hispanic mustache, and his closely shaven head. He was wearing a black T-shirt. He aimed his gun and blasted at him six times. One of the bullets hit him in the ribs. The five other occupants in the vehicle ducked and screamed while the driver began going in and out of consciousness. One of the back passengers grabbed the wheel until they finally crashed into a wooden fence by their apartment a long ways from the base of the hill.

The driver was hospitalized. He told officers that the one who shot him was named "Rico Martinez." He knew him because he had seen him about five or six other times during gang fights.

Rico and I began the court process. We had several routine hearings before I got some bad news. Rico had been shot and was in the hospital. When I was able to speak with him, I found out what had happened. He had been sitting on the porch at his house when two hooded men opened the gate to his yard, walked toward him on the sidewalk to his front door, and then asked him one question: "Are you Rico Martinez?" Right after he responded in the affirmative, one of the men pulled out a sawed-off shotgun from underneath his coat-jacket and fired at him twice. Rico jumped up and escaped from the retaliation with a minor wound to his hip and to his thumb. Roles had changed. Now he was the hunted.

This injured attempted murderer was my client to defend.

Head of the criminal justice program at a local college, Ron Fey sat across from me at his large desk inside his tight office filled with books. He was a big, athletic man with a bald head and full mustache. He had hired me as an instructor to teach criminology—the study of crime and why people commit it. I was planning on being a criminal defense lawyer when my primary job as a judge's law clerk was completed.

With a polite smile, he asked, "Taylor, how do you justify *defending* criminals if you're a dedicated member of The Church of Jesus Christ of Latter-day Saints?"

I was almost dumbfounded by the question. It struck me as "does not compute." Did I just hear him ask that question? Was he implying that *true* disciples of Christ are duty-bound to *fight* criminals? Are they to *attack* the enemy?

My answer essentially expressed the idea that, to me, the question should naturally be in the reverse: how could a careful follower of Christ feel comfortable *condemning* and *combating* any person, especially criminals and sinners?

In the following chapters, I would like to elaborate on the answer I gave Mr. Fey because the question is not uncommon. I distinctly recall another experience later when I went to a Church member's home for a fancy party. The platinum blonde–haired host looked at me as she wrinkled her nose. "How do you like working with the *scum of the earth*?" So, I shouldn't be in the business of defending "scum"?

These experiences and others show that many faithful and devoted religious people, as well as sincere spiritual people, question the morality of defending individuals who are clearly guilty of crime. They even question the morality of defending those who are only probably guilty of crime—those who are only accused of crime. I write specifically to you who have similar questions.

I want to address this legitimate concern and I hope to resolve it by using legal, spiritual, and religious standards and principles, many of which you should be familiar with, but may have never connected together in certain ways. The answer is divided into two main parts relating to the two types of clients: the guilty and the accused. You will see throughout the book these two main themes. One theme deals with levels of certainty for the accused while the other deals with compassion for the guilty.

When it comes down to it, I am giving you my legal and spiritual testimony on the matter, which legal and religious aspects interrelate heavily.

This book is *not* written for the spiritual pansy or the religiously averse, except to provide these kinds of people with perspectives that they have probably never before considered as carefully as they should have.

Major portions of this book will incorporate legal standards, generated by the intellectual giants of the United States Supreme Court, and relate them to God-delivered knowledge found in ancient and modern scripture in order to arrive at the answer to Mr. Fey's question.

2

PERSONAL HISTORY: THE HEART OF A SOCIAL WORKER AND THE MIND OF A LAWYER

How can *I* defend the guilty? Let me give you some background about myself to help answer that question. It requires a discussion of my own spiritual development and development in the law.

Initially, as a pre-teen and young teenager, I found it more appealing to love God (the first great commandment) than love others (the second great commandment). The first commandment is recorded in both the New Testament and the Old Testament. In Matthew 22:36–38, we read, "Master, which is the great commandment in the law? Jesus said unto him, Thou shalt love the Lord thy God with all thy heart, and with all thy soul, and with all thy mind. This is the first and great commandment." In Deuteronomy 6:5, we see it recorded as, "[T]hou shalt love the Lord thy God with all thine heart, and with all thy soul, and with all thy might." When it comes to the second great commandment, we see it in both portions of the Bible. In Matthew 22:39–40, it reads, "And the second is like unto it, Thou shalt love thy neighbour as thyself. On these two commandments hang all the law and the prophets" and in Leviticus 19:18, it states, "Thou shalt not avenge, nor bear any grudge against the children of thy people, but thou shalt love thy neighbour as thyself: I am the Lord."

To me, loving God meant being obedient to commandments and rules. It meant studying the word of God carefully, pondering truth deeply, praying intently, and going to church as a faithful Latter-day Saint. These inward, more self-involved efforts were the only spiritual labors that were truly fulfilling to me at that time. Outward shows of genuine compassion to others did not interest me—in fact, the idea was repulsive. I just wanted to love God, not others.

During this time of loving God, I remember being told that "people problems" are the hardest problems. At times, this was repeated in the context of discussing future occupations that closely involved people. Perhaps it sunk in because during this time as a teenager, I gained a strong interest in becoming an astrophysicist—a job with only astronomical problems rather than people ones.

The more I developed spiritually and drew closer to God's ways, however, the more this maxim about people problems did everything *but* discourage me from wanting to take on those problems. While I grew in my knowledge of truth and conviction of what is morally right, life became purposeful if it was filled with meaningful challenges to overcome. If people problems were truly the hardest problems, then that's where I wanted to focus my life's pursuits.

Figuring out how to solve people problems, such as mitigating the plight of the poor or taking proactive efforts to help people suffering from various difficulties, was less of a challenge to overcome and more of a sincere wish that I wanted for the sake of *their* welfare. The motivation came from altruism and sincere compassion rather than some personal competition to try and conquer a challenge. I developed an understanding and appreciation for the intrinsic value of goodness in every person. This change came naturally the more and more I came to love God.

The internal change from solely inward-involved righteousness to including outward-directed goodness led me to pursue a major in psychology. I became interested in why people acted and reacted the way they did, especially when their behavior was not easily explained. What basis was there for, and what influences contributed to, a person choosing to do one thing over another thing in the same or similar circumstances as another person who chose differently? With a criminal law and spiritual perspective, the question becomes: beyond the wrong act itself, are there components of accountability for the wrongful act that make the person less responsible for it? Do we have to take into account how each person was raised, their good and bad experiences, the stressors and people in their lives, and any conditions beyond their control to mitigate the degree of guiltiness a person has for doing the wrong?

Accountability for the wrong act had to be a component, or else this next question would never even be a factual issue: why do good people sometimes choose to break social rules and harm others while other equally decent people refrain from doing so? Is there an explanation? Could it be that in these instances, there is some contributing influence beyond the person's control? If there is, is it a satisfactory explanation? If so, then (from a psychological perspective) with this knowledge, could I generate a solution to the apparent behavioral disorders? Could I then decrease the number of victims that result from the deviant behaviors?

I wanted to know the answers to these questions because my heart went out to the victims, no matter who they were. I realized that the wrongdoers were often victims themselves. They were victims acting out. Instead of acting out appropriately, though, they were acting out improperly. But their actions and reactions did not determine the sympathy I felt for them. Their status as victims did. I wanted to help *all* victims—regardless of their own conduct. A victim is a victim.

Shortly before graduating from Brigham Young University with a bachelor's degree in psychology, I looked into a master's of social work (MSW) degree for a major. I thought this was where I could put my psychology background to its most practical use for helping others. I also found that my heart was in social work.

I pursued this course of social work until my dad was driving me to BYU one day and suggested an option that excited me. He told me of a degree called a "JDMSW," or juris doctor masters of social work. What was a *juris doctor*? He told me it was a law degree and it could be combined with a social work degree and done at the same time. That sounded like a powerful degree for good. After a lot of thought, prayer, consideration, and soul searching, I determined that a JDMSW is what I wanted. Unfortunately, BYU didn't offer a JDMSW. They were in the experimental stages of offering one, but that kind of untested program wasn't going to work for me.

As I explored the JDMSW option, I felt inspired that, and came to believe, I personally would be a stronger influence for good in helping others as an attorney than I would as a social worker. As a result, I decided to go to law school for a JD degree first and then, perhaps, pursue an MSW degree to tack on later. Even if I didn't get an MSW, I thought that as a lawyer I could help social workers' clients and perhaps do the good for them that I hoped to do as a social worker.

After considerable examination of law schools, I calculated that California Western School of Law in San Diego was the best school for me, especially with its Innocence Program that liberates the incarcerated who were wrongly convicted. I also figured that with my average LSAT (Law School Admission Test) score and above average undergraduate GPA this school would not only accept me but would also offer me a scholarship. My confidence in this was strong enough that I didn't apply to any other law schools. But when others heard of all my eggs being in one basket, they convinced me that it was a bad idea. I then applied to three schools on the East Coast, to the University of Utah, and to the University of California Davis, as backup plans.

As predicted, California Western accepted me and offered one of its best scholarships if I decided to attend their school. The scholarship included full tuition for the first year and half tuition for each of the second and third years. (As a side note, all the other schools rejected me; I, of course, took the California Western offer.)

Law school was an extraordinary experience. While attending my first semester, I especially loved criminal law because it was deeply moral. I collected quotes from my professor that appeared to me to have distinct spiritual or moral meaning. Let me cite a few that have particular relation to this book.

Professor Jaeger, in my Criminal Law class of 2002, stated: "Much of what we do and don't do isn't mediated by knowledge—we don't need to know for certain that a person is in their true hour of need before we react."

He also said, "Belief is grounded in something, unlike fantasy, which isn't grounded in anything. If you can't point to something in the public, observable world, then we would say that that belief is not good enough. Ungrounded belief wipes out malice but establishes that the person is profoundly deluded."

Like a true criminal defense lawyer, he also declared at another time, "The law should attempt to improve our frailties, not acknowledge them."

A year later, I had a Torts class, taught by Professor Flint. Torts is the broad area of law that covers nearly all the wrongs people can do (except violation of contracts) that other individuals, rather than the state, can sue them for. It is civil in nature. Professor Flint said, "Knowledge in practice is more certain than knowledge in theory."

Quoting Justice Holmes, the former US Supreme Court justice, he said, "A page of history is worth a pound of logic."

In my constitutional law class, I read a case from the early 1800s that developed the United States Supreme Court's ability to make judicial decisions on more than just federal matters, but also state matters. Justice Story in that case explained:

> This is not all. A motive of another kind, perfectly compatible with the most sincere respect for state tribunals [or state supreme courts], might induce the grant of appellate power [for the Supreme Court of the United States] over their decisions. That motive is the importance, and even necessity of uniformity of decisions throughout the whole United States, upon all subjects within the purview of the constitution. *Judges of equal learning and integrity, in different states, might differently interpret* a statute, or a treaty of the United States, or even *the constitution itself*: *If there were no revising authority to control these jarring and discordant judgments, and harmonize them into uniformity, the laws, the treaties, and the constitution of the United States would be different in different states, and might, perhaps, never have precisely the same construction, obligation, or efficacy, in any two states. The public mischiefs that would attend such a state of things would be truly deplorable*; and it cannot be believed that they could have escaped the enlightened convention which formed the constitution. What, indeed, might then have been only prophecy, has now become fact; and the appellate jurisdiction must continue to be the only adequate remedy for such evils.[1]

Other classes gave me a basic understanding of highly practical information for everyday living in society. I felt everybody should go to law school to get this fundamental knowledge.

Then my grades came back.

A letter came with them that stated, "We invite you to withdraw." What? The school was inviting me to withdraw from law school based on too many poor grades. Criminal Law was one of them; I had performed miserably, and it was only a one-semester class, so there was no chance of performing better in it later.

I went to a school administrator to discuss the issue of *not* withdrawing. She told me that based on decades of experience that the school had had with students in my situation, I would be unable to raise my overall law school grades in order to meet the minimum first year requirements to stay in law school there. Her certain prediction was that I would inevitably be kicked out at the end of my first year and never be able to return to California Western.

I knew a number of law school friends in similar circumstances that decided to withdraw so they could return about two or three years later to California Western. But I refused to withdraw, even though I was told failing law school was the most likely—if not guaranteed—outcome. My plan was to beat the odds. And I believed I knew how to do that.

I began implementing my plan by relying in part on a friendship I had first formed when I initially came to Church activities in San Diego. His name was Spencer Hill. He was an elder in the priesthood, like me, and had served an honorable, two-year, full-time mission for the Church. We had served in different areas of the world, but our missions were the same: sincerely sharing the fulness of the Gospel of Jesus Christ with as many people as we could and encouraging them to follow Christ by being baptized into His Church, the one He fully authorizes as His own, and also to make the change of living Christ's teachings an enduring lifestyle for them.

With the trust I had in Spencer as a true friend and in the priesthood that he held, I asked him for a priesthood blessing. He laid his hands on my head and pronounced a blessing under the inspiration of the Spirit, ending it in the name of Jesus Christ. When he was done, I sincerely believed it was actually a blessing from Jesus

Christ. In the blessing, *He* told me that I would "fix" my grades. I understood the word *fix* to mean more than simply get grades good enough to stay in law school that year. I understood it to mean that I would get grades good enough to fix my scholastic position with the school so I would never be in danger of getting kicked out or of failing again.

With tremendous effort on my part, palpable stress every moment of every day burning inside my chest cavity (for at least two months into the second semester), extra tutoring, concerted prayers at night that included mentally rehearsing some of what I had learned that day, and developing outlines of the concepts I was learning, along with divine intervention on God's part, the priesthood blessing came true, precisely as I had understood it. The genuine miracle took place. In fact, when I showed my grades to the school, I was told that they had never before seen such a dramatic improvement as mine. I had done significantly better in classes I had performed poorly in and did fair to well in the others.

My grades put me into a position where I was no longer in danger of ever being kicked out or of failing. Significantly, in my contracts class where I had scored the lowest out of everyone in my first semester, I ended up scoring the highest in the second semester and received an award for it. Then, in my second year of law school, I was selected, based on grades, to be the large group tutor of about seventy first-year contracts students. In a separate, classlike setting for about an hour, I reviewed with them what had been taught each week, answered their questions, and added my own techniques for teaching the material in order that the students might more effectively learn it. At the final close of that tutoring time, the first-year student who scored the highest that semester had been attending my tutoring sessions. Not every first-year contracts student attended because the tutoring was offered only as a strongly recommended course after regular school hours, not a mandated class.

Before becoming a tutor, but after the enormous struggle of my second semester of law school, I developed the mind of a lawyer. I began thinking like a lawyer instead of a social worker. My heart, however, was still that of a social worker.

Note

1. *Martin v. Hunter's Lessee*, 14 U.S. 304, 347-348 (1816). Emphasis added.

3

THE JOB THAT STRIPS AWAY NEARLY ALL LIMITS ON OPTIMISM

Shortly after obtaining my Juris Doctor degree from California Western School of Law, I married my exceptionally impressive wife, Jamie, whom I had pursued off and on (mostly on) for over four years. We lived in La Mesa, an adjacent city to San Diego, while I worked for an employment law attorney. For family reasons, Jamie and I ended up moving back to Utah. Once in Utah, I had to prepare to take the Utah bar examination in order to become an attorney who was licensed to practice law in Utah. I got a hold of some BYU students' outlines and some books and studied on my own without attending a bar preparation course to help me.

At the same time, I began looking for work as a law clerk in different law firms. I had considered doing personal injury law or medical malpractice, but decided that I wanted to do juvenile law to help children and youth—much like a social worker might do. Eventually, I got hired at Dallas & Westover doing some juvenile law work. I wasn't aware that juvenile law is mostly just a watered down version of criminal defense. The vast majority of the work at Dallas & Westover, though, was pure criminal defense. But criminal law was a class I had failed.

Adjusting to doing work in an area that I was supposedly weak, I thought that I might gain a renewed interest in criminal law and acquire some skills in the process.

My hope came true.

I loved criminal defense! It was fascinating. I discovered that of the differing kinds of civil attorneys that I had been thinking of being, becoming an attorney in the criminal area was truly what I wanted.

Initially, while working at Dallas & Westover (and then later at the Fourth District Court in Provo as a law clerk for a judge), I thought I would first become a criminal defense lawyer and then move on to become a prosecutor—this, I thought, would make me an expert in criminal law and be a better prosecutor by first "swimming with the sharks" (defense lawyers), so to speak, and then beating the sharks (as a prosecutor).

During this general period, I passed the Utah bar examination the first time without having taken any bar courses. Then I worked for the judge for over a year, taught criminology and other classes at a local college, and then got hired on by a family law attorney, who let me develop my own criminal defense practice on the side. After about nine months with the family law firm, I branched off entirely to start my own practice as a criminal defense lawyer in a small business called, The Advocate Attorney, LLC (see www.TheAdvocateAttorney.com). I was also working on a 501(c)(3) non-profit organization with my wife, Jamie, that she and I cofounded to help those suffering from Epidermolysis Bullosa (EB), a rare skin disorder, become self-reliant, give back to the community, and live fulfilling lives. (The organization's name is the United Survivors of Epidermolysis Bullosa (USeb). See www.ebsurvivors.org for more details.)

Since becoming a criminal defense lawyer, I have learned to see my role as threefold: (1) protect the innocent who are wrongly accused of crime(s); (2) insure that the guilty are treated fairly and not penalized more than they deserve, which would violate their Eighth Amendment right under the U.S. Constitution to be free from "cruel and unusual punishments"; and (3) keep the "good guys" good, who are our law enforcement officers by preventing them from achieving their proper ends when they use *illegal means* to accomplish those goals.

From the varied experiences that I've had in the different areas of the law, I am convinced that criminal defense helps me best apply my heart—the heart of a social worker—because of the three roles that I have. Criminal defense, like no other area of the law, allows me to be as optimistic and positive about people and humanity as I can be with the proper basis for doing so (which basis I'll explain more in the proceeding chapters).

In contrast, I don't have a job that requires me or leads me to believe people, especially those accused of crimes, are all criminals to some degree or are dishonest individuals, like prosecutors end up believing by the accusatory nature of their job. Rather, I can see criminals or alleged criminals each as inherently good people who are telling me the general truth. I get to view them as people who, for a variety of reasons, even reasons sometimes beyond their control, may have gotten into trouble and done something wrong. And then I get to be their advocate. I get to protect their rights, fight for them against false accusations, voice the mitigating circumstances of their cases, speak about accountability (or culpability), and present their descriptions of what happened in the most forcefully convincing way I can. In doing so, I get to help many of them obtain either justice or leniency.

4

LENIENCY VS. MERCY

In the last chapter I spoke about helping my clients receive either justice or leniency. Usually, you hear justice and mercy coupled together. So, why do I say "leniency" and not "mercy"? It's because the two concepts of leniency and mercy are materially different, making mercy inapplicable to criminal legal situations. Let me explain why.

In a human-based system of justice, the only break people receive is leniency. In a God-based system of justice, the break people receive is mercy because the Lord Himself suffers or has suffered the predetermined punishment for our sins (and crimes). God's system of justice is real justice because in all fairness, His set punishment for sins (or crimes) must be paid by someone who can take responsibility for the wrong. That someone is the perfect Lord God Jesus Christ, who suffered the pain for our sins and crimes against divine law beginning in Gethsemane and continuing on until He gave up His life on the cross.

But in our system of justice, and when the break from penalty is applied, no single person receives the predetermined punishment for the crime committed by the defendant. The crime committed simply goes unpunished, or at least not fully punished, because we apply leniency and are not as hard on the person as the law says we justly could be. This commonly happens through plea agreements for those who are guilty of more but admit to less. Plea agreements form the vast majority of resolutions in criminal cases. Unfortunately, though, many innocent people wrongly suffer reduced penalties through these plea agreements in order to avoid the risk of suffering a much greater penalty if a jury or judge mistakenly believed them guilty of all the crimes they were accused of.

I think the best consolation for times like these when the innocent wrongly endure punishment for something they didn't do is found in 1 Peter 2:20–21: "For what glory is it, if, when ye be buffeted for your faults, ye shall take it patiently? but if, when ye do well, and suffer for it, ye take it patiently, this is acceptable with God. For even hereunto were ye called: because Christ also suffered for us, leaving us an example, that ye should follow his steps." We are following Christ's example when we are unfairly punished for crimes we didn't commit and we take it patiently—that's where the glory and acceptability is.

Other unfairness happens in the effort to capture criminals who are actually guilty of wrongdoing. Consider an example in Utah from 1988. The facts clearly established, and there was no dispute, that "the police conducted an illegal roadblock in . . . Utah, on a section of Interstate 15." About fifteen law enforcement officers were "assigned to operate the roadblock. They were instructed to check driver's licenses and vehicle registrations and to look for any criminal activity." This kind of roadblock is illegal because, among other things, it seized every driver who would be passing by. The description of the event continues:

> A car driven by Dennis Shoulderblade stopped at the roadblock. Leaning in the car window, an officer requested the car's registration and valid identification from Shoulderblade and his passenger, Lemuel Small. Both produced identification, but the car was not registered to either occupant. Small explained that the car belonged to his friend. The officer radioed dispatch to confirm the vehicle's registration and to check the occupants' driver's licenses. While waiting for confirmation, the officer interrogated Shoulderblade and Small. . . . He also asked if they had any alcohol, firearms, or drugs in the car, and they both replied in the negative. According to the officer, what Shoulderblade and Small were doing was "entirely lawful."

Even though the officer did not see anything out of the ordinary, he continued to detain them and "asked if he could look in the vehicle." There was no legal requirement to let the officer do this. They could have said, "No," and the officers would have had let them go on their way. When an officer asks for it, refusing to give consent for a search is not an indication of guilt. The fact the officer asks you for consent is an indication that he's on a fishing expedition for illegal items. If an officer has legal justification to search, he doesn't need to ask you for consent to do it. However, in this case, "Small consented" and "substantial quantities of drugs, drug paraphernalia, firearms, and cash were found." They were both arrested. "Prior to their joint trial, both Shoulderblade and Small moved to suppress the evidence obtained in the search. The trial court denied the motions, and the jury found Shoulderblade and Small guilty."

Both men appealed the guilty verdicts, arguing that the "evidence seized from the vehicle should be suppressed," which would have dismissed the case before trial, because Small's consent to have the vehicle searched was "not sufficiently attenuated to dissipate the taint of the illegal roadblock." In other words, the police's exploitation of the illegal roadblock to gather evidence was what wrongfully produced the evidence that led to the guilty verdict.

In the end, the Utah Supreme Court agreed with the fully guilty, criminal defendants that "because the temporal proximity and apparent purpose of the traffic stop indicate exploitation of the illegal roadblock with no intervening circumstances, the consent to have the vehicle searched," which consent usually allows searches, "was not sufficiently attenuated," or the consent was *not* given far enough away in time to make it a separate event from the illegal roadblock, which, if it were far away enough in time, it would "dissipate the taint of the illegal roadblock," or take away the illegal influence of the roadblock and allow the consent for the search to be valid. Without the influence of the illegal roadblock taken away, though, that influence extended into Small's consent for the officer to search his vehicle, making his consent invalid and making the search illegal.[1]

As in the prior example, there are times when fully guilty criminal defendants receive complete leniency and are not punished at all for something they are clearly guilty of. The reason is that the

Constitution of the United States acknowledges certain inherent rights and socially contracted upon rights. When some of those rights are violated by the "good guys," who are our police and law enforcement officers, then our human-based system of justice in America says the guilty can go free.

The guilty go free in these instances because our system of justice absolutely will not tolerate people in authority using illegal means to accomplish their good ends. Their good ends are supposed to be catching the "bad guys" and preventing victims. But they cannot use illegal methods to achieve those ends. They cannot be the "bad guys" in the process of catching people that are violating the law and, thereby, victimize the law breaker and end up as hypocrites. The law does not allow regular people to take the law into their own hands and it also does not allow law enforcement to take the law into their own hands. Simply put, in America, the ends do not justify the means. Everyone must follow the law. Period.

But, you might wonder, isn't this morally corrupt? Isn't it better to prevent victims at all cost—even the cost of accidentally punishing the innocent while ensuring that the guilty don't go free (an approach to justice other cultures in the world sometimes take)? Isn't there a realistically better way of administering justice than allowing the guilty people to go entirely free when law enforcement commits crime or other wrongs against these criminals? The short answer is no. History has demonstrated that the only way to keep law enforcement from becoming organized crime, which is far more dangerous than one criminal going free, is to allow the officers to fail in their purpose of catching the "bad guys."

Essentially, we punish only law enforcement when they violate certain laws and rights of individuals—*even* individuals who are guilty of crime. These protections typically relate to a person's Fourth and Fifth Amendment rights about illegal searches, seizures, and incriminating statements. The punishment to law enforcement comes in the form of excluding evidence against the defendant. The exclusion typically gets the case totally dismissed, even though the evidence shows the defendant is guilty. The so-called punishment to the police that allows the guilty to go free is corrective and the police will conform (for the most part) or they can't perform their work.

The Utah Supreme Court explained a good reason for this exclusionary rule—excluding such illegally obtained evidence "prevents the courts from becoming a party to wrongdoing and maintains public confidence in the integrity of governmental action."[2] The federal court stated another reason: "the purpose of the exclusionary rule is to deter future unlawful police conduct and thereby effectuate the Fourth Amendment guarantee against unreasonable searches and seizures."[3] The U.S. Supreme Court further explained:

> The rule is calculated to prevent, not to repair. Its purpose is to deter—to compel respect for the constitutional guaranty in *the only effectively available way*—by removing the incentive to disregard it. . . . [T]here are[] many unlawful searches of homes and automobiles of innocent people which turn up nothing incriminating, in which no arrest is made, about which courts do nothing, and about which we never hear. Courts can protect the innocent against such invasions only indirectly and through the medium of excluding evidence obtained against those who frequently are guilty.[4]

Martin Luther King Jr. explained the danger sought to be avoided by the exclusionary rule in saying, "Injustice anywhere is a threat to justice everywhere." Seemingly small injustices by the police toward even a single criminal threaten the justice of everyone because of the potential for their small injustices to become widespread. The injustice must be stopped wherever it is found, even if it is from the "good guys."

The indirect "punishment" to the police for their misconduct is unequal because our system only punishes the potentially greater wrongdoer (law enforcement) while the lesser wrongdoer (the criminal) goes completely free. Also, the punishment given to the potentially greater wrongdoer is not as severe as it justifiably could be. But because it works in its corrective purposes, our system of justice simply leaves the remaining punishment up to the lesser wrongdoer to inflict on the potentially greater wrongdoer in the form of a state or federal civil rights lawsuit. The burden to sue the wrongdoing police officer (who is the potentially greater wrongdoer because of his tight unity with other officers, all of whom enforce the law and who could also follow in the wrongdoing police officer's footsteps and then become *organized crime*) for violation of the criminal's civil rights is on the shoulders of the guilty criminal defendant.

The next section of the book, section two, will provide the necessary foundation for understanding how *knowledge* of the facts or *knowledge* of the truth should play a vital role in the views you take on people *accused* of crime. The main discussion about proper treatment toward the actually *guilty* criminals will be in the third section of this book. These three sections work together to comprehensively answer the question about how can I defend criminals and be religiously moral at the same time.

Notes

1. *State v. Shoulderblade*, 905 P.2d 289 (Utah 1995)
2. *Id.*
3. *United States v. Kember*, 648 F. 2d 1354, 1367 (Court App. Dist. of Columbia 1980).
4. *Elkins v. United States*, 364 U.S. 206, 217-218 (1960). Emphasis added. Internal quotations omitted.

SECTION II

EVIDENTIARY STANDARDS AND STANDARDS OF TRUTH, DEGREES OF CERTAINTY, AND SPIRITUAL TRUTH SCRUTINY AND THEIR APPLICATION TO THE ACCUSED

5

EVIDENTIARY STANDARDS

One of the reasons why I believe our system of justice incorporates leniency is because it understands that discovering the actual truth about what happened is very difficult. It also recognizes that honest mistakes can be made in that process.

The challenge in any legal case, criminal or civil, is finding out what happened and who is or isn't liable or guilty for it. Once the facts are established to an acceptable degree of certainty, then a court with authority can assign that civil liability or criminal guilt to a specific person.

The process of discovering the facts takes time and effort. Significant amounts of time and effort are and should be put into the process of discovering the facts for the purpose of safeguarding the accused. The American jurisprudence attitude is that it is better to let guilty people go free than to punish the innocent. We must protect people from being wrongly convicted of crime.

In determining what the facts are, courts allow differing amounts of certainty and uncertainty about those facts. The law recognizes at least seven evidentiary standards of truth or degrees of certainty.[1] From the least certain to the most, they are as follows:

- Hunch
- Reasonable, articulable suspicion (RAS)
- Probable cause (PC)
- Preponderance of the evidence (the most common civil standard) (PE)

- Clear and convincing evidence (the highest civil standard, which is used in cases that may take away a parent's rights to his or her own child, for example) (CCE)
- Proof beyond a reasonable doubt (the criminal standard) (BARD)
- Absolute knowledge

Let me provide you with my criminal defense–attorney understanding of the legal definitions of these degrees of certainty, their application to criminal cases, and what I understand to be the rough percentage degree of certainty each starts out at on a 100 percent scale:

> **0%**: "Hunch" is a gut feeling based on so little evidence that a person cannot verbally pinpoint what it is that makes him or her believe or want to believe something, yet they do anyway.
>
> **25%**: "RAS" or "reasonable, articulable suspicion" is when there is at least some degree of evidence that leads a reasonable person to *suspect* something is or is not true (or that criminal activity is afoot) ***and*** that person can genuinely verbalize what the evidentiary basis is.
>
> **40%**: "PC" or "probable cause" is when there's enough evidence to lead a reasonable person to *believe* something is or is not true (or that a crime was committed by a specific individual).
>
> **51%**: "PE" or "preponderance of the evidence" is when there's enough evidence to *convince* a reasonable person that something is *more likely* true than untrue (or that the defendant is *more likely* to be the criminal of the crime than not, that is, if this standard were to be applied in a criminal context).
>
> **70%**: "CCE" or "clear and convincing evidence" is when there's such a high degree of evidence that a reasonable person would have a *strong conviction* that something is

clearly more true than probably false, or vice versa (or that a defendant is clearly most likely guilty of a specific crime than anyone else, if applied in a criminal context).

95%: "BARD" or "beyond a reasonable doubt" is when there's such a significant amount or quality of evidence that a reasonable person would not be able to entertain any doubt as to the truth or falsity of something, except for unreasonable doubts (or the person knows what took place almost as well as if he or she were present when the allegedly criminal event took place).

100%: "Absolute knowledge" is when a reasonable person actually knows something in its entirety from their own experience and senses (or they are present when the allegedly criminal event takes place, they are *fully* aware of what happened and who did it and *exactly* how accountable the guilty one is for it, and they accurately comprehend the *entire* event).

Let's distinguish a couple of the above evidentiary standards. In typical *civil* cases, when a complete set of facts is missing, we use reason to supply the missing bits of information and/or to interpret the evidence we have. This allows us to arrive at a final conclusion. We only have to be about 51 percent certain of the truth of what happened in order to treat our conclusion as 100 percent true. This certainty is the "PE," or "preponderance of the evidence," or the more-likely-than-not standard. It is the fourth degree of certainty above.

Consider the case of "Dr. Melvin Cook" who "invented slurry explosives" and how the preponderance of the evidence standard played into his situation. Justice Oaks wrote for the court in this *civil* (not criminal) case:

> For twenty-two years, he devoted his efforts to the manufacture and sale of the product [slurry explosives]. His son, Merrill Cook, managed slurry companies for about 5 years. With this experience, the Cooks began preparations to establish a new business . . . in Minnesota and Utah. The Minnesota plant [would

include] three silos for the storage of ammonium nitrate pellets, an essential ingredient of slurry.[2]

A dealer promised to supply the parts to construct these explosives containers and that these "parts would be adequate to construct the silos." The parties signed a contract and the dealer gave the Cooks a written statement that delivery of the parts would be on "8/17 or 8/18." On August 17, 1978, the Cooks were notified by telephone that "all the parts were loaded and ready for shipment." Then, in reliance on this promise, "Cook released a $33,660 check to the dealer as payment for the parts. However, the expected shipment did not arrive at the Minnesota plant until the week of September 8, 1978, and many of the ordered parts were missing or defective."

Ultimately, the "last of the parts did not arrive" until about a year later on "August 3, 1979" and the containers for the explosives couldn't be made until September of 1979. This was eight months after the date Cook had planned to begin production of the explosives. "The plant experienced its first sales and a net profit of $23,022 in October 1979. Thereafter, its average monthly net profit through the first 13 months of operation was $35,650." In Cook's lawsuit against the dealer for delays in completing the Minnesota plant, the jury awarded compensatory damages, among other things. When it was taken on appeal, it was argued that "the compensatory damages were . . . not established with sufficient certainty nor shown to be foreseeable" as required for granting an award of money to compensate the one harmed. The court analyzed the problem by stating, "Lost profits must be established with . . . sufficient certainty that reasonable minds might believe from a *preponderance of the evidence* that the damages were actually suffered."[3]

The court decided against the argument on appeal that the compensatory damages were *not* proven with sufficient certainty. The Utah Supreme Court affirmed the original jury award to the Cooks of $56,908 because they *were* adequately proven as lost profits by a preponderance of the evidence. This nearly $60,000 amount was given to the Cooks to compensate them for the profits they supposedly lost because of the delay.[4]

Could the court really know that the Cooks actually lost $60,000 in profits during the delay when the nature of business is not always so predictable? The answer is no. And that's okay. The court has to make an educated guess. It can't know. There are too many variables that can make one educated guess about as good as another. And in the *civil* world, that's okay so long as the guess is more likely true than not from a reasonable person's perspective.

In another way of expressing the preponderance of the evidence standard, civil cases allow us to entertain as much as 49 percent doubt (both reasonable and unreasonable) as to what actually happened and who is actually liable for the wrong and still be comfortable assigning total responsibility—which can mean thousands and thousands of dollars, as in the Cook example. This is the rational approach to solving problems. Many of these problems, in all practicality, cannot otherwise be resolved because of the lack of evidence or other difficulties. As in the Cook example, there is no way to know for certain how its business would have actually performed if it had started as planned eight months earlier. Market conditions are always fluctuating and little changes in one thing can lead to dramatic effects in another. The Cooks might have performed substantially better and should have been compensated by the dealer more than $60,000 or substantially worse, meaning the dealer should not have had to pay the Cooks anywhere near $60,000. There's no way to know with complete certainty in examples like the Cook case. But, this is the beauty of reason—its solving power.

Or so people think.

Notes

1. *See generally United States v. Sokolow*, 490 U.S. 1 (1989) (discussing hunch, RAS, PC, and PE), Addington v. Texas, 441 U.S. 418 (1979) (discussing CCE and BARD), and United States v. Jewell, 532 F. 2d 697, fn. 6 (9th Cir. Ct. App. 1976) (discussing absolute knowledge).
2. *See Cook Associates*, Inc. v. Warnick, 664 P. 2d 1161 (Utah 1983).
3. *Id.* Citations and quotations omitted. Emphasis added.
4. *Id.*

6

EVIDENTIARY STANDARDS AND THE REALITY OF REASON

From various experiences, legal and otherwise, I have become firmly convinced that too many people overvalue "reason" and what is "rational" or "logical" to the point of ignoring better standards of truth. One of the common abuses of these standards of reason is in the area of spirituality and religion, which spills over into people's everyday lives. Broadly speaking, the area of spirituality includes how we consider and deal with other people on a daily basis and how we view and treat social organizations, such as religion, politics, and education.

To help demonstrate how people's refusal to use higher standards of truth harms their ability to accurately perceive the world and the people in it, I'll focus on the particularly sensitive areas of spirituality and religion. Discussing how we deal with spirituality and religion can augment our abilities to correctly judge and rightly treat (1) those charged with crime and (2) those convicted of crime.

In the areas of spirituality or religion, many people combine secular concepts with spiritual ones. They do this by saying that what is true and right (the spiritual concepts) has to be reasonable and logical (the secular concepts). To a degree, they're right. But there is a sad truth about reason that is reflected in my favorite quote from law school that courts also frequently acknowledge: "reasonable minds can differ."[1] This truth is very clearly expressed in the quote introduced earlier in this book about the reasonable minds of judges and the need for a United States Supreme Court as a revising authority for the differing judgments they would make:

> Judges of equal learning and integrity, in different states, might differently interpret . . . even the constitution itself: If there were no revising authority to control these jarring and discordant judgments, and harmonize them into uniformity, . . . the constitution of the United States would be different in different states, and might, perhaps, never have precisely the same construction, obligation, or efficacy, in any two states. The public mischiefs that would attend such a state of things would be truly deplorable.[2]

Because of this fact that reasonable minds can differ, I've grown to distrust reason as a tool for finding actual truth.

The strongest powers of reason can do nothing more than discover that which is "more likely" or "most likely" true because reason is what you use when you don't have knowledge. By itself, reason can never determine *with total certainty* that which is true. Please note, reason *is* capable of determining what is true—it can get it right. But what it can't do is determine truth with total certainty; reason cannot guarantee that it is absolutely correct in what it determines is true. Reason is a dangerously low standard for determining actual truth because "reasonable minds can differ" on the truth of a single matter and yet still be *reasonable.* How do you like that? Contradictions about the truth. Contradictions about what is true. Yet both positions are considered reasonable and, therefore, correct. This reality helps explain Justice Holmes's observation that a "page of history is worth a pound of logic." It takes a lot of logic or reason to equal a small portion of experiential knowledge. I refer to "history" as "experiential knowledge," but even history is not always reliable.

We have to be careful about overvaluing history as a source of truth, too. History is "his-story." Essentially, it's a "story" that's only as believable as the person telling it. Because even eyewitness accounts of *current* events are frequently wrong, misinterpreted, and inaccurate, the eyewitnesses from the *past* historical events are just as susceptible to the same errors. Historical eyewitnesses, however, present a more severe problem—they die and we never have the chance to cross-examine them in order to determine the full accuracy of their account. Without further exploration, their recorded account remains as if it is the absolute truth about what happened when it could very well be mistaken, inaccurate, incomplete, or simply untrue. The true value of history, though, is in the portions of knowledge that are gained through experience.

Take, for example, the logic of the ancient mountain hiker and his perspective:

1. The mountain is standing still.
2. The round sun is rising, moving over the mountain, and then setting.
3. The sun repeats this motion the next day, every day.
4. At night, the moon and stars also move through the dark sky, similar to the sun.
5. The mountain is attached to the flat earth, which also does not move.
6. The flat earth, therefore, is stationary while the sun and stars rotate around it.

We know that's not true. So what went wrong? Wasn't the logic correct? The hiker's reasoning was rational but flawed. He failed to include all the relevant evidence upon which to make a conclusion. He used reason as a substitute for his lack of knowledge and did not see that there is, in fact, an entire solar system of spherical bodies that rotate around the similarly-shaped sun. But from what he could observe with his eyes, it didn't appear that way, which led him to faulty, but rational conclusions. History is replete with people using reason that ultimately proves faulty because it fails to consider all the circumstances.

As a result of the weaknesses inherent in them, reason and its logical conclusions about absolute truths end up giving people a false sense of security in the accuracy of their beliefs or faith. Because people frequently use logic and reason as substitutes for well-earned knowledge to determine truth for their spirituality, they also tend to use them in judging and condemning others. They fail to see and consider all the relevant circumstances in determining culpability. When judging and condemning others, however, people should be satisfied with nothing less than knowledge of the critically important details because inaccurate judgments and/or mistaken condemnations have the power to drastically ruin another person's life, who doesn't deserve the ruin.

Let's discuss knowledge for a moment. What is knowledge? Some may say "knowledge is knowledge" and there is no difference in the amount of certainty to it. But, as I see it, there are at least four differing degrees of certainty in what we deem "knowledge." From least certain to most, there is (1) academic or theoretical knowledge, which is "knowledge in theory"; (2) knowledge based on the lack of reasonable doubt from all the evidences, which is indirect knowledge; (3) experiential knowledge or "knowledge in practice," which is direct knowledge; and (4) absolute knowledge, which is complete *and* transcends any error and lacks every degree of uncertainty, however minute.

By themselves, reason and logic, *at best*, can only amount to the first category—knowledge in theory or academic knowledge—if that at all. And, as my Torts professor accurately observed, "Knowledge in practice is more certain than knowledge in theory." And the more certain the knowledge, the better it is. The farther away we depart from logic and reason and the closer we come to knowledge in practice or even absolute knowledge, the better off we are in having accurate understandings of truth. In the criminal context and the area of spirituality, as we approach the knowledge that lacks reasonable doubt, we can better avoid mistaken judgments of others and more easily treat them right, even though our knowledge may not be equal in certainty to experiential or absolute knowledge.

The second category of knowledge is very important as the more objective criminal defense standard: "proof beyond a reasonable doubt." In criminal cases, the amount of facts and evidence has to objectively prove the truth of what happened to such a high degree of certainty that there is no room for even moderate amounts of reason. There's no room for rational conjecture, educated guesses, reasonable speculations, logical imaginations, properly-based creativity, or even knowledge in theory or plain academic knowledge alone. Why? Because in each of those instances, there will be a degree of doubt, which is reasonable; in the criminal matter context, there's absolutely no room for *any* and *all* reasonable doubt concerning what crime happened and who is guilty of the crime. The evidence has to be enough in quality and quantity to eliminate the doubt that all the relevant, necessary evidence of the circumstances may not have been presented. This is to protect the innocent from being falsely convicted of crime. If there is any reasonable doubt, then we give the defendant the benefit of the doubt and let him or her go free as a person completely innocent of the criminal accusations.

This very high criminal standard of evidence doesn't require absolute knowledge of what happened. It's such a high standard, however, that the only doubts that can exist are unreasonable doubts.

The great advantage of this standard of truth or evidence is that, in theory, it protects innocent people from having to suffer the harshest of all penalties that our society metes out—the criminal penalties. In practice, it prevents a lot of (but not all) innocent people from being wrongly incarcerated, deprived of their liberty, severely penalized with harsh fines, and protects them from being wrongly committed to treatment programs and institutions.

The following is from a case where proof beyond a reasonable doubt protected a person from a conviction for second-degree murder. "Phyllis Ady, age 15, was reported missing at 1:00 a.m. on December 13, 1977." Just over two-and-one-half years later "a man . . . uncovered a human skeleton by a row of trees along a fence line in the large backyard behind his rented home." The skeleton was almost three feet beneath a "mound of earth" covering a "wooden trap door." The trap door went to "an old carrot pit," where the skeleton lay. The police concluded from the position of the skeleton that "the body had been placed in the pit on its chest with the hips bent forward and the legs and arms folded over the back of the body."

Along with the skeleton, the police "discovered a ring, a jacket, a sweater with a pin attached, blue jeans, female underclothing, and a pair of boxer shorts." The medical examiner concluded that "the skeleton was that of a female between 14 and 17 years of age, approximately 5 feet 2 inches in height (plus or minus 2 inches)." The left forearm had a "thickened area indicating a healed fracture." The teeth contained "no dental work." Neither the time *nor the cause of death* could be determined from the skeletal remains. The descriptions of the skeleton matched those of Phyllis Ady.

One of Phyllis's acquaintances was accused of murdering her.

He was the defendant. "At the time Phyllis disappeared, she and the defendant were both 15 years of age. They lived about a half block apart. . . . They attended the same school, but they apparently did not have a dating relationship." Phyllis's aunt testified that "before December 12, 1977, the defendant had been to their home on only one occasion, the day before, when he merely came to the door to inquire if Phyllis was home."

As she was being driven around, Phyllis asked her driver to let her off at the defendant's home. Later that night, the driver returned to the defendant's house. "[W]hen the defendant answered the door, [the driver] asked about Phyllis's whereabouts." The defendant replied that he didn't know where she was and that "she had left him and gone with a blond long-haired fellow" that the defendant didn't know. At 1:00 a.m., the driver reported Phyllis missing.

On the evening of December 12, about four hours before Phyllis was reported missing, the defendant had telephoned his sister in Las Vegas. He told her that "he was getting a hassle at home and in school, and he wanted to come down." He phoned again the next morning, and his sister picked him up and drove him back to Las Vegas, where he stayed for about four days.

The court explained, "Aside from whatever inference might be drawn from the fact that defendant was the last person seen with Phyllis before she disappeared and the fact that he left Cedar City the day after she disappeared, the only evidence of the defendant's guilt of murder in the second degree were statements he made" later to various people.

When the defendant was in Las Vegas, his sister and her husband "heard him screaming in the night, before midnight." Concluding that he was having a nightmare, "they took him into the kitchen to talk about it." The defendant's sister testified in court what the kitchen conversation was about:

> We asked Johnny what his nightmares [were] about. He said he was having a nightmare about walking with a girl and she slapped him and that's all he remembered, and then waking up[,] taking a bath and her folks, the girl's folks[,] pounding on the door wanting to know where she was. Later he said he thought he had hurt or killed a girl, but he wasn't sure.

In context, and by its literal terms, "this testimony clearly referred to the content of Johnny's (defendant's) dream, although the last quoted answer might be subject to the interpretation that it referred to an actual occurrence."

The defendant's brother testified that he went to the home in Las Vegas during his brother's four-day visit to tell him that "the Cedar City Police were looking for him to question him about the disappearance of a young girl." The brother said to the defendant he was going to return him to Cedar City. The testimony from the brother continued as follows:

> Well, he proceeded to tell me that he was walking through a field with—I took it as a young girl. He didn't say what girl or who it was, but she slapped him. He blacked out. And then he goes on from there to say about the dreams . . . [W]hen he blacked out and he started to dream that he—his words were he thought he hurt her. He thought he might have killed her.

The court explained, "In context, it is clear that the statements" related in the testimony of the defendant's brother "were entirely concerned with defendant's dream and not with actual events. This was further emphasized in the cross-examination."

The only other evidence of the defendant's guilt came in the testimony of a girl who had dated the defendant in Las Vegas or California in the winter of 1980, more than two years after Phyllis disappeared. She testified that during one of their conversations, the defendant told her that he "had gotten into a fight with a girl in Utah. He mentioned no names, dates, or other details." His statement about this event, as described in the witness's testimony was "so inconsequential to this witness that she said it 'just passed through one ear and out the other.' In short, it could have referred to any of a variety of real or exaggerated events in the dating life of a teenager." There was no other evidence of guilt.

Based on this, the jury found the defendant guilty of second degree murder. The Utah Supreme Court, however, decided that "the evidence was not sufficient to prove, beyond a reasonable doubt, that defendant caused Phyllis Ady's death." Even if the evidence proved that defendant caused her death, "it was manifestly insufficient to prove that he did so 'intentionally or knowingly,' as was charged in this complaint for murder in the second degree."[3] He was released from incarceration. The case exemplifies the danger of using only the "more likely than not" standard for truth when determining guilt.

Like in the prior case of Phyllis's death, if used in a criminal context, the lower civil standards of preponderance of the evidence (PE) or clear and convincing evidence (CCE) would sentence a great many more innocent people to the penalties that significantly alter, if not shatter, their personal lives as well as the lives of their loved ones. This greater amount of sentencing would happen because reason can be wrong—and frequently is—and yet be reasonable and treated as totally true. The jury had reasons to believe the defendant killed Phyllis, but it also had many more reasons to doubt it, and the Utah Supreme Court had to reverse the jury's decision because it was not based on "proof" that is "beyond a reasonable doubt."

With this basic understanding about the differences between reason and knowledge, we can explore the gamut of certainty degrees more in the next chapters, which is extremely important in accurately judging people as criminals and in determining how to treat them.

Notes

1. *Adrian School Dist. v. MPSERS*, 582 N.W. 2d 767, 769 (Mich. 1998).
2. *Martin v. Hunter's Lessee*, 14 U.S. 304, 348 (1816).
3. *See State v. Petree*, 659 P. 2d 443 (Utah 1983).

7

TYING THE EVIDENTIARY STANDARDS TOGETHER WITH THE DEGREES OF CERTAINTY ABOUT SPIRITUAL TRUTHS

I WANT YOU TO TRY AN EXERCISE BEFORE YOU CONTINUE. ON THE next two pages, check "yes" or "no" to the statement next to the choices. Then mark how certain you are that you are correct when agreeing or disagreeing with the statement.

Have you marked your answers? They should have varied between, and including, "Don't know" and "Know." I wanted you to try this experiment to help demonstrate one of the themes of this book—it is not whether something *is* actually true or not (the left hand columns of "yes" and "no"), but the focus is on how *certain* you are (the right hand columns) that it actually is or is not true. The two concepts of truth and certainty of the truth are significantly different, but similar enough that people often confuse them.

You will find much more "truth" in the world, whether secular or spiritual, if you allow yourself to use lower standards of certainty. This does not mean you are truly finding what is actually true. It only means you are accepting ideas, concepts, and spiritual or secular matters as true that will inevitably include false ones or inaccuracies. And, many times, this is tolerable and in some cases even commendable.

If, on the other hand, you insist on using the higher standards of certainty, then you will find much less "truth" in the world because it is sometimes impossible to obtain the higher degrees of certainty about some things. For example, if you marked that you "know"

Yes	No	Statement of Truth or Falsehood	How Certain?				
			Don't know	Suspect	Trust or Believe	Most Likely True	Know
		Your mother loves you					
		Your first grade teacher liked you more than her average student					
		Some chocolate once a day is beneficial to you					
		The world is facing an upcoming ice age					
		You have a Father in Heaven					
		You will live at least ten more years					
		The President of the United States is looking out for you					
		People in Namibia experience depression					
		You were excited to come to earth before you were born					
		You know how tall you are—in meters					
		You frequently dream at night					

Yes	No	Statement of Truth or Falsehood	How Certain?				
			Don't know	Suspect	Trust or Believe	Most Likely True	Know
		Your best friend had a stomach ache at about nine years old					
		You've felt or experienced God's influence before					
		You're dad might have cheated on a test in high school					
		Newton devised the law of gravity after an apple hit him on the head					
		You would have developed a markedly different personality if you had been adopted at three years old and raised by the Bushmen of Africa					
		You would not have developed any significantly different personality if you had been born three thousand years ago					
		The sun is a huge ball of compact, burning gas					
		DNA controls only your physical characteristics, not how you think					
		You have a spirit within your body					

the sun is a "huge ball of compact, burning gas," you may be right from one angle of academic knowledge, but technically wrong from a couple of other perspectives. Basic academic knowledge says it is a "huge ball of compact, burning gas." More advanced academic knowledge would say it is a "huge ball of plasma, not gas." Plasma is the fourth state of matter. Even burning gas cannot achieve the heat that plasma produces. Plasma is so hot that the atoms within it move fast enough to knock electrons out of orbit, making it electrically charged and susceptible to magnetic influence. Gas is not usually electrically charged or susceptible to magnetic influences.

From another perspective, you cannot "know" the sun is a "huge ball of compact, burning gas" because (1) it doesn't look like gas—gas floats away; and (2) you've never touched it personally to know for yourself what it's made of. You probably haven't even looked at it for more than a few seconds at a time. Thus, in reality, you probably just trust that the sun is what scientists say it is or you are as much as "more certain" that it is what they say it is than you are "uncertain" about it, which is the preponderance of the evidence (PE) standard or the more-likely-than-not standard. You'll never know for absolute certainty until, perhaps, the next life.

The exceptionally high criminal standard for being certain of truth beyond a reasonable doubt comes close to fulfilling, if not fulfills, a standard for being certain of truth that is found in the ancient Hindu text called the *Bhagavad-Gita*. It states, "Without direct experience, one has to rely on theory and concepts; theorizing and make-believe have no place in one's spiritual career."[1]

This statement expresses in a conclusionary way why I strongly disfavor using reason for finding truth. Reason is more often than not tantamount to theory and sometimes even make-believe. The conclusion is that reason or rationality should have no place in your spiritual career. The basis supporting this conclusion is what was previously discussed: reason cannot determine with absolute certainty what "is" true, only what is "more likely" or "most likely" true.

Let's explore the Hindu scripture's quote a little further. What is our spiritual career? I submit that all of us have the spiritual career of making the lifelong effort to find, accept, and live by what is actually true. And reason, theory, and make-believe are clearly not sufficient.

The career's salary for our sincere and dedicated efforts is the eventual discovery of actual truth with high degrees of certainty, along with the reception of all the benefits that come with knowing truth and living by it.

Just like in criminal cases, theory and make-believe should have no place in the process of discovering truth. As the ancient Hindu text emphasizes, to be fully successful in these endeavors, we each absolutely have to have direct experiences (which, generally speaking, is the third category of knowledge: "knowledge in practice")—but direct experiences with what? When it comes to spiritual and religious matters, we must have "direct experience" with the Source of all truth. For criminal matters, it means that the evidence must so outweigh the use of reason that, really, the only reason that exists is *un*reasonable doubt.

If we have direct experiences with the Author of all truth, then we are gaining absolute knowledge, the fourth category of knowledge, because "[w]hat greater witness can you have than from God?" (D&C 6:23), or what more certain knowledge can you obtain than that received directly from Deity? There would be no question as to the accuracy of the knowledge that He directly gave you because He is a God of truth.

As the Brother of Jared stated, "Yea, Lord, I know that thou speakest the truth, for thou art a God of truth, and canst not lie" (Ether 3:12). Thus, you can have *complete certainty* when God gives you knowledge by *direct* experience with Him. In other words, you have absolute knowledge. Absolute knowledge leaves no room for even the smallest doubt—no doubt that the message might have been delivered inaccurately by Him, no doubt that it might be incomplete from what it was supposed to have been, no doubt that there might be a mistake, and no doubt that you might be being deceived by Him. We'll discuss more on why this is in chapter eleven.

Even experiential knowledge, on the other hand, is always subject to the remote possibility that what you experienced was not what it seemed to be. For example, I had knowledge by experience that a popular song used the word "humbling." I heard it every time I listened to the lyrics of the song. I had no doubt. There was no question in my mind. However, as my wife, Jamie, listened to the song, she heard "unbelievable." Once she pointed it out to me, I realized my experiential knowledge was wrong. I now heard it; the word was "unbelievable." And that's how I felt too—it was "unbelievable" that my experiential knowledge could have been so wrong. But absolute knowledge from the Perfect Supreme Being does not suffer from this vulnerability.

For our spiritual careers, we need our own experiences with the Divine on some level, whether direct or indirect. Otherwise, we end up easily doing one of two things, or a combination of both: (1) we rely on concepts that we've only read or been told about and that we haven't proven as true, which is a form of hearsay; or (2) we make up our own truths like a preschool child playing make-believe. Then my criminal law professor's quote about ungrounded belief, fantasy, and being deluded certainly comes into play.[2]

There is danger in relying on either of these two alternatives (or combining them), instead of seeking, waiting for, and relying on direct experience at some level, because doing so in a spiritual context will inevitably disrupt how we view criminals and harm how we end up treating them.

Let me offer an illustration. In our spiritual and religious lives, it is completely okay to say, "I have faith in Christ," or "I believe the Church is true." These are expressions of hope mixed with some level of uncertainty. We follow, or should follow, as if we're 100 percent sure. Because in our spiritual and religious lives this devotion is acceptable, and even laudable, we tend to think it is also okay to say, "I believe he or she is truly guilty" and then treat the person as if he or she is, in fact, guilty. There is uncertainty, though, and yet we use gap-fillers, such as reason and logic to make up for the missing amounts of certainty so we can feel justified in treating the person as guilty—"Well, he's a gang member, so he must be guilty; she's an unwed mother, so she must be immoral; he's an illegal immigrant from Afganistan, so he must be a terrorist." Essentially, we are engaging in make-believe with these rational, rule-of-thumb, common sense conclusions. It's make-believe because our general rules of thumb or common sense fills in the gaps where we don't have knowledge on the matter, knowledge of facts such as "he's actually been struggling to leave the gang and the gang is now blackmailing him; actually, she was married and then had her child ten months later; actually, he's illegal only because his student visa expired and he's doing his best to renew it and make for himself a better life in a country with freedoms that he cherishes."

Before I demonstrate with experiences (or knowledge in practice) how make-believe can make people arrive at draconian judgments of others that I had with my own client (see chapter 18), I need to establish a foundation of how all of the evidentiary standards of truth can be converted into differing degrees of spiritual certainty of truth, and vice versa. The relations between the two help show how unnatural it is for ordinary, spiritual people to use the secular reasonable doubt standard to judge someone.

When we understand how to arrive at a high certainty of truth and, on the other hand, when we realize we have not achieved that high degree of certainty, we can then treat *accused* people more properly. With this in mind, defending *these* people is much easier and appropriate. We must unwaveringly fight to protect the accused, no matter how guilty they look, in case we misjudge them as criminals and fail to protect the actually innocent. Let me develop this concept better in the following chapters.

Notes

1. *The Bhagavad Gita*, translated by Jack Hawley, Ph.D. (New World Library, 2001), 50.
2. "Belief is grounded in something, unlike fantasy, which isn't grounded in anything. If you can't point to something in the public, observable world, then we would say that that belief is not good enough. Ungrounded belief wipes out malice but establishes that the person is profoundly deluded." Professor Jaeger, Criminal Law, 2002.

8

THE LAW'S EVIDENTIARY STANDARDS AND ALMA'S DEGREES OF SPIRITUAL CERTAINTY

For millennia, spiritual people and religious leaders have taught on the subject of faith. As a result, faith is commonly viewed as an exclusively separate concept from the secular degrees of certainty. (Remember the secular degrees are [1] hunch; [2] reasonable, articulable suspicion [RAS]; [3] probable cause [PC]; [4] preponderance of the evidence [PE]; [5] clear and convincing evidence [CCE]; [6] proof beyond a reasonable doubt [BARD]; and [7] absolute knowledge [AK]).

It is significant to note that the Book of Mormon was written by many prophets, who had direct experiences with God, and that it teaches much about faith. It even shows how faith can be developed into absolute or "perfect" knowledge.

Alma the younger taught particularly on faith and knowledge. His background may indicate why. He was the first chief judge of the land (see Mosiah 29:42, 44) and had a roughly eight-year term as chief judge (about 91–83 BC),[1] which means he had a significant amount of legal experiences (see Alma 7:1–2). In his spiritual life, he also had direct experiences with angels from God that taught him truth (see Alma 8:14–18, 10:10, and 17:2).

Interestingly, Alma, who probably had the most legal experiences of all the prophets, goes into great detail on the subject of experimenting with faith to find out what is true and, thereby, gain perfect knowledge on the matter. He treats faith as a degree of certainty about the truth.[2] He explains this aspect of faith about nine years after his term as chief judge had ended,[3] giving him plenty of time to relate the virtues of his work to spiritual concepts when preaching to others. Alma's description of the process of moving from faith to absolute knowledge is much more sophisticated than what a cursory reading of the text would show. There appears to be deep legal parallels, which is consistent with Alma having served as a judge of legal matters and possibly many criminal ones. In Alma 32:17–19, the prophet explains:

> Yea, there are many who do say: If thou wilt show unto us a sign from heaven, then we shall *know of a surety*; then we shall *believe*.
>
> Now I ask, is this *faith*? Behold, I say unto you, Nay; for if a man *knoweth* a thing he hath no cause to believe, for he knoweth it.
>
> And now, how much more cursed is he that knoweth the will of God and doeth it not, than he that only believeth, or only hath *cause to believe*, and falleth into transgression? (Emphasis added)

As I read these verses, I glean five, separate, yet highly interrelated degrees of spiritual certainty about truth. I put them in what I understand to be the lowest degree of certainty to the highest:

- "Cause to believe"
- "Believe"
- "Faith"
- "Know"
- "Know of a surety" by "a sign from heaven"

Before we continue, we need to consider Alma's "cause to believe" concept. It's striking. "Cause to believe" is a term found in no other prophets' writings in all of scripture, ancient or modern, and yet it is found frequently in some of the greatest legal opinions of all time, beginning firmly in the twentieth-century with *Terry v. Ohio*:

> Officer McFadden, on the basis of his experience, 'had reasonable *cause to believe* . . . that the defendants were conducting themselves suspiciously' . . . [and] reasonable *cause to believe* might be armed. . . . We conclude . . . today that

> where a police officer observes unusual conduct which leads him reasonably to conclude . . . that criminal activity may be afoot and that the persons with whom he is dealing may be armed and presently dangerous . . . he is entitled . . . to conduct a carefully limited search . . . [for] weapons which might be used to assault him.[4]

The standard of evidence created in this 1968 United States Supreme Court decision was the reasonable, articulable suspicion degree of certainty, as indicated later in the following U.S. Supreme Court Decision: "In *Terry*, we held that an officer may, consistent with the Fourth Amendment, conduct a brief, investigatory stop when the officer has a *reasonable, articulable suspicion* that criminal activity is afoot."[5] Thus, legally, "cause to believe" and "reasonable, articulable suspicion" (RAS) are synonymous. I have put a thermometer diagram later in this chapter to illustrate the intriguing parallel comparison between the scriptural "cause to believe" from the prophet and first chief judge Alma and "reasonable, articulable suspicion," a modern evidentiary concept from the legal giants of the United States Supreme Court. The thermometer is a fitting illustration to convey the reality of the differences between degrees of certainty. We are not simply certain or uncertain. This simplistic, binary way of thinking is what causes a lot of mistaken judgments. There are multiple degrees of certainty, all of which must be understood and appreciated before making important decisions about either spiritual or secular truth.

Alma continues and I find a slightly different list of degrees of certainty about the truth, which may not all be separate degrees, but different descriptions for the same level of certainty:

> And now as I said concerning *faith*—faith is not to have a *perfect knowledge* of things; therefore if ye have faith ye *hope* for things which are not seen, which are true.
>
> And now, behold, I say unto you, and I would that ye should remember, that God is merciful unto all who *believe* on his name; therefore he desireth, in the first place, that ye should believe, yea, even on his word. (Alma 32:21–22, emphasis added)

The list is as follows:

- "Believe"
- "Hope" in "things . . . which are true," but "not seen" (or not *proven* to give *knowledge*)
- "Faith"
- "Perfect knowledge"

Going on in Alma 32:26–27, the degrees of certainty are explained in more detail, and at least two of them are the same degrees of certainty:

> Now, as I said concerning *faith*—that it was not *a perfect knowledge*—even so it is with my words. Ye cannot *know of their surety* at first, unto perfection, any more than faith is a perfect knowledge.
>
> But behold, if ye will awake and arouse your faculties, even to an experiment upon my words, and exercise a *particle of faith*, yea, even if ye can no more than *desire to believe*, let this desire work in you, even until ye *believe* in a manner that ye can *give place* for a portion of my words. (Emphasis added)

The list is as follows:

- "Desire to believe"
- "Particle of faith"
- "Believe"
- "Give place"
- "Faith"
- "Know of [a] surety"
- "Perfect knowledge"

Then, in the next verses (Alma 32:28–34), I find the list in even greater detail, which I've written out below in a more organized, outline format. It's also important to note how interconnected these degrees of certainty are—they flow into each other smoothly from one degree of certainty to another so well that it's sometimes hard to see the change without looking and considering carefully:

> Now, we will compare the word unto a seed. Now, if ye *give place*, that a seed may be *planted in your heart*, behold, if it be a

true seed, or a good seed, if ye do not *cast it out* by your *unbelief,* that ye will resist the Spirit of the Lord, behold, it will *begin to swell* within your breasts; and when you feel these swelling motions, ye will begin to say within yourselves—It must needs be that this is a good seed, or that the word is good, for it beginneth to *enlarge my soul*; yea, it beginneth to *enlighten my understanding,* yea, it beginneth to be *delicious* to me.

Now behold, would not this increase your *faith*? I say unto you, Yea; nevertheless it hath not grown up to a *perfect knowledge.*

But behold, *as* the seed *swelleth,* and *sprouteth,* and beginneth to *grow,* then you must needs say that the seed is good; for behold it swelleth, and sprouteth, and beginneth to grow. And now, behold, will not this *strengthen your faith*? Yea, it will strengthen your faith: for ye will say I *know* that this is a good seed; for behold it sprouteth and beginneth to grow.

And now, behold, are ye *sure* that this is a good seed? I say unto you, Yea; for every seed *bringeth forth unto its own likeness.*

Therefore, if a seed groweth it is good, but if it groweth not, behold it is not good, therefore it is cast away.

And now, behold, because ye *have tried the experiment,* and planted the seed, and it swelleth and sprouteth, and beginneth to grow, ye must needs *know* that the seed is good.

And now, behold, is your *knowledge perfect*? Yea, your knowledge is *perfect in that thing,* and your *faith is dormant*; and this because *you know, for ye know that the word hath* swelled your souls, and ye also know that *it hath* sprouted up, that your understanding doth begin to be enlightened, and your mind doth begin to expand.

I. Unbelief

A."Cast[ing] it out"

II. Belief

A. "Giv[ing] place"

B. "Plant[ing] in [the] heart"

III."Faith"

A. Feeling the *beginnings* of (from the language "begin to" and "beginneth"):

1. Swelling motions within breast
2. Enlargement of the soul
3. Enlightenment of the understanding
4. Deliciousness

IV. Strong Faith (from the language "*strengthen* your faith")

A. Witnessing the consistent *continuation* of (from the language "*as* the seed . . ."):

1. Swelling
2. Sprouting
3. Growing

V. Knowledge

A. Experiencing the *completion* or near completion of (from the language "every seed bringeth forth unto its own likeness" and having "*tried* the experiment" and "you know, for ye know that the word *hath* . . .") the word having:

1. Swelled the soul
2. Sprouted and causes understanding to be enlightened
3. Grew so the mind expands

VI. Perfect Knowledge (from the language "yea, your knowledge is *perfect*")

A. Development of knowledge to "perfect" knowledge "in that thing," or one highly specific area

What I find remarkable is that the degrees of certainty that Alma described above parallel the evidentiary standards that have been developed by modern legal giants over years of highly sophisticated and genuinely complex case law. On the following pages is the consolidated list of the multiple degrees of spiritual certainty, as discussed by Alma in the cited verses, placed in a parallel comparison with the evidentiary standards of truth, or secular degrees of certainty:

0. Unbelief A. Casting out	**0. Non-certainty**
I. Desire to believe (Alma 32:27) A. Exercising a particle of faith (Alma 32:27)	**1. Hunch**
II. Cause to believe (Alma 32:18)	**2. Reasonable, Articulable Suspicion**
III. Belief (Alma 32:22,27) A. Give place (Alma 32:28) B. Planting in the heart (Alma 32:28)	**3. Probable Cause**
IV. Faith (Alma 32:29) A. Hope in unseen, but true things (Alma 32:21) B. Feeling the beginnings of: (Alma 32:28) *1. Swelling motions within breast (Alma 32:28)* *2. Enlargement of the soul (Alma 32:28)* *3. Enlightenment of the understanding (Alma 32:28)* *4. Deliciousness (Alma 32:28)*	**4. Preponderance of the evidence**
V. Strong Faith (Alma 32:30) A. Witnessing the *continuation* of: (Alma 32:30) *1. Swelling (Alma 32:30)* *2. Sprouting (Alma 32:30)* *3. Growth (Alma 32:30)*	**5. Clear & Convincing Evidence**

VI. Knowledge/To Be Sure (Alma 32:30-31, 33) A. Experiencing the *near* completion of: (Alma 32:30–31,33) *1. Swelling of the soul (Alma 32:30–31,33)* *2. Sprouting that causes understanding to be enlightened (Alma 32:30–31,33)* *3. Growth of the mind expanding (Alma 32:30–31, 33)*	**6. Beyond a Reasonable Doubt**
VII. Perfect Knowledge Know of a surety by signs (Alma 32:17, 34) A. Experiencing the *final* completion of: (Alma 32:31, 33–34) *1. Swelling of the soul (Alma 32:34)* *2. Sprouting that causes understanding to be enlightened (Alma 32:34)* *3. Growth of the mind expanding (Alma 32:34)* B. Faith is dormant (Alma 32:34)	**7. Absolute Knowledge**

The parallels are a very surprising coincidence. Notice from above, for example, how "faith" parallels "preponderance of the evidence." Preponderance of the evidence, or the more-likely-than-not standard, is the one of two civil standards that is most commonly used. When civil courts use it, they only need enough evidence to make them more certain about the truth than uncertain, and then they treat their certainty as 100 percent certain, and act on it by issuing a binding order that a person must follow. Isn't it interesting how well the concept of faith parallels preponderance of the evidence?

Here's the parallel from another perspective—when it comes to faith, isn't it also true that we are supposed to be at least more certain than uncertain about the truth (have "evidence of things not seen," Hebrews 11:1, the more-likely-than-not standard), treat our faith as if we're 100 percent certain of the truth (just as we do in civil courts after the more likely than not standard is met), and then act accordingly (just as civil courts do when entering a binding order on the liable party)?

It is my understanding that the Lord does not want us to wait for perfect knowledge about the truth before we act on it. Recall also Professor Jaeger's comment, "[W]e don't need to know for certain that a person is in their true hour of need before we react." The reason may be that in acting on what we have faith in, we discover for certain whether it is true or false, just as Alma describes, and similar to what Christ described during His mortal ministry: "If any man will *do* [the Father's] will, he *shall know* of the doctrine, whether it be of God, or whether I speak of myself" (John 7:17, emphasis added).

You may worry, though, about starting this process out with false beliefs. Starting out with false beliefs should not be a deep concern because if our sincere beliefs end up being wrong, there is no punishment in it—we are free to "worship[] Almighty God according to the dictates of our own conscience, and [we] allow all men . . . [to] worship how, where, or what they may" (see Article of Faith 11). It was the same anciently: "Now there was no law against a man's belief; for it was strictly contrary to the commands of God that there should be a law which should bring men on to unequal grounds" (Alma 30:7). Further, as Alma explained, if we plant the seed of belief in a spiritual claim that is actually wrong, then the seed won't "grow"—in other words, you will discover by your own experience that "it is not good," and you are then to disbelieve it or "cast [it] away" (Alma 32:32).

As long as we follow the dictates of our own conscience, then we will be led to more truth: "the word of the Lord was unto them . . . line upon line; *here a little, and there a little*" (Isaiah 28:13, emphasis added). As we follow the truth to which we are guided, then we will be led to more truth, as Isaiah 58:11 states, "And the Lord shall guide thee *continually*." Speaking of this continual guidance, the prophet Alma promised, "[H]e that will not harden his heart, to him is given the greater portion of the word, until it is given unto him to know the mysteries of God until he know them in full" (Alma 12:10).

If, however, we are sincerely mistaken about the truth and then act wrongly and discover our error, then God is abundantly merciful. Saul's conversion is a great example. He imprisoned and consented to the murder of Christians (Acts 26:10), sincerely thinking he was doing right. Christ appeared to him and corrected his misbehavior and was abundantly merciful by even calling him to be His witness and do His work (see Acts 9).

Similarly, Christ allows us the chance to repent of our wrong act, do good, and be treated by Him as if we had never made the mistake. Isaiah 1:18 teaches that though your "sins"—not just your sincere mistakes, but even your sins—be red like "scarlet," they will be "white" as snow with the Lord's cleansing power.[6] Alma himself alluded to the value of faith/belief/cause-to-believe over knowledge because of the less severe punishment a person receives when acting against it instead of knowledge. He said, "And now, how much more cursed is he that knoweth the will of God and doeth it not, than he that only believeth, or only hath cause to believe, and falleth into transgression?" (Alma 32:19).

SEVEN DEGREES OF CERTAINTY

The seven degrees of certainty listed numerically in the left column have corresponding legal and spiritual certainty levels in the following two columns. The legal and spiritual certainty levels each have names for roughly the same numerical degree of certainty. See Alma 32:18–34

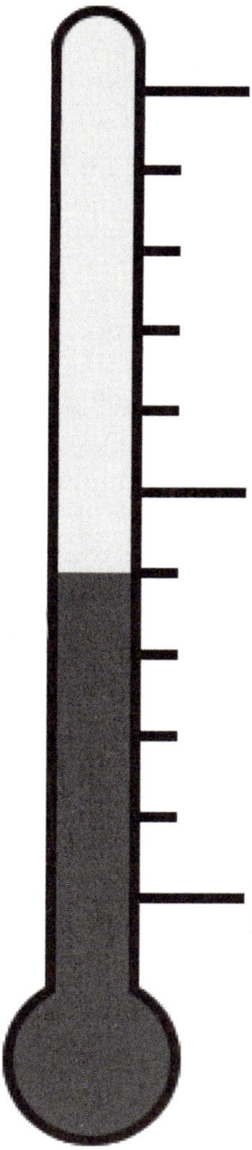

DEGREE	LEGAL CERTAINTIES	SPIRITUAL CERTAINTIES
100%	ABSOLUTE KNOWLEDGE	PERFECT KNOWLEDGE
95%	BEYOND A REASONABLE DOUBT	KNOWLEDGE
70%	CLEAR AND CONVINCING EVIDENCE	STRONG FAITH
51%	PREPONDERANCE OF THE EVIDENCE	FAITH
40%	PROBABLE CAUSE	BELIEF
25%	REASONABLE ARTICULABLE SUSPICION	CAUSE TO BELIEVE
0%	HUNCH	DESIRE TO BELIEVE

Notes

1. See Alma 1 (especially v. 2) and 4 (especially v. 20).
2. "Faith" is a much more complex concept than simply being a degree of certainty about truth, but Alma focuses on this particular aspect of faith more than what I can find any other ancient prophet has done.
3. See Alma 32—"About 74 BC" compared to "83 BC" when he finished his term as chief judge in Alma 4.
4. *Terry v. Ohio* 392 U.S. 1, 8, 30 (1968), emphasis added.
5. *Illinois v. Wardlow*, 528 US 119, 123 (2000), emphasis added.
6. The context of the scripture is also important: "Wash you, make you clean; put away the evil of your doings from before mine eyes; cease to do evil; Learn to do well; seek judgment, relieve the oppressed, judge the fatherless, plead for the widow. Come now, and let us reason together, saith the Lord: though your sins be as scarlet, they shall be as white as snow; though they be red like crimson, they shall be as wool. If ye be willing and obedient, ye shall eat the good of the land: But if ye refuse and rebel, ye shall be devoured with the sword: for the mouth of the Lord hath spoken it" (Isaiah 1:16–20).

9

INTRODUCTION TO THE TESTS AND THE RATIONAL BASIS TEST

In the previous chapters, we acknowledged how truth can be either secular or spiritual. We learned of the differing degrees of secular certainty that we can have about the truth[1] and also differing degrees of spiritual certainty about the truth.[2] Quite interestingly, the degrees of secular certainty about truth and the degrees of spiritual certainty about truth can be seen to roughly parallel one another. From this perspective, the various degrees of certainty in both types of truth simply have different names for the same degree of certainty.[3]

SPECIFIC REQUIREMENTS MUST BE MET IN ORDER TO ACHIEVE EACH LEVEL OF CERTAINTY

Even though the discovery of the potential parallels between secular and spiritual certainties is significant, the parallels are only *descriptions* of what reality is concerning degrees of certainty. They say nothing about how to achieve those particular degrees of certainty.

The next step, then, is to find out the *requirements* for arriving at these differing degrees of certainty about the truth. When the requirements are met, we can know at what level of certainty our convictions are. This concept will become clearer as we go through each of the three tests that I have yet to explain. The *methods* for meeting these requirements are what the Word of God already speaks of, such as the method of prayer to the Creator of our Spirits in order to find out truth,[4] so I won't go into detail here except to eagerly encourage all people to sincerely apply those methods.

Once we compare our spiritual experiences to the requirements set out for particular degrees of certainty about the truth, we will know how certain we are and how uncertain we may be. As we become familiar with measuring our convictions in this way—which you may find strange or awkward at first—we can apply roughly the same secular requirements for the judgments we make toward people on a daily basis. This will help us know how certain or uncertain we actually are about our judgments toward them. Knowing how certain we are in the judgments we make about people accused of crimes relates directly to the basic question of this book: "Taylor, how do you justify *defending* criminals if you're a dedicated member of The Church of Jesus Christ of Latter-day Saints?"

The question doesn't distinguish between the guilty and the accused, but lumps them both together as "criminals." We need to mentally separate the two before we continue. The reason for this is that the justification for defending those actually *guilty* of crime is different than the justification for defending those merely *accused* of crime. First, let's discuss the justification for defending those merely accused of crime.

DEFENDING THE ACCUSED: JUSTIFICATIONS

Part of the answer is that it is highly appropriate to defend and protect an accused person, whom you don't know is guilty, because final judgments about accused sinners or alleged criminals should only be made when we have a high degree of certainty about their culpability. This is a loaded statement. Let's break it down.

First, what are the requirements for achieving the high degrees of certainty about any truth—the truth of a person's culpability, for example?

Second, who really is a sinner or a criminal and what is culpability? Culpability means guiltiness. The answer to who really is a sinner or criminal is beyond the scope of this book, but it is an important question to keep in mind when judging people. Essentially, though, the answer relates to the accountability question mentioned briefly in chapter two.

Third, what are final judgments? The short answer is that they are judgments we make that do not change even when other pertinent information comes along.

I left the first question unanswered. To answer it, let me show you below, beginning with the most basic set of requirements and then progressing on to the most advanced set of requirements for achieving the various degrees of certainty about spiritual truth.

THE EQUAL PROTECTION TESTS DEVELOPED BY THE U.S. SUPREME COURT

Using constitutional analysis developed by the United States Supreme Court for equal protection issues, I've come up with what I call "Spiritual Truth Scrutiny." Before I describe my own tests, let me show you the legal tests that they are based on as described by the United States Supreme Court:

> The Equal Protection Clause of the Fourteenth Amendment commands that no State shall 'deny to any person within its jurisdiction the equal protection of the laws,' which is essentially a direction that all persons similarly situated should be treated alike . . . [T]he courts have themselves devised standards for determining the validity of state legislation or other official action that is challenged as denying equal protection. The general [*rational basis*] rule is that legislation is presumed to be valid and will be sustained if the classification drawn by the statute is *rationally related to a legitimate state interest*. . . . The general rule gives way, however, when a statute classifies by race, alienage, or national origin. These factors are so seldom relevant to the achievement of any legitimate state interest that laws grounded in such considerations are deemed to reflect prejudice and antipathy—a view that those in the burdened class are not as worthy or deserving as others. For these reasons and because such discrimination is unlikely to be soon rectified by legislative means, these laws are subjected to *strict scrutiny* and will be sustained only if they are *suitably tailored* [or *necessary and involving no less restrictive alternatives available*] to serve a *compelling state interest*. . . . Legislative classifications based on gender also call for a heightened standard of review [*intermediate scrutiny*]. That factor generally provides no sensible ground for differential treatment . . . . A gender classification fails unless it is *substantially related to a sufficiently important governmental interest*.[5]

The constitutional analysis tests, then, are as follows based on the idea that for equal protection, "all persons similarly circumstanced shall be treated alike."[6] "Equal Protection" does not mean treating everyone the same regardless of their situations. It means taking into account some of the distinguishing features or circumstances of one group of people that would make it unfair to treat them the same as another differing group of people. Accordingly, the law will make rules and regulations that apply to different classes of people because of their differing circumstances. These laws that apply to one group over another have to be carefully examined by the following tests to make sure they provide equal protection of the people.

1. **Rational Basis Test**: For most classes of people treated differently by the law than other classes of people, the unequal treatment will be Constitutionally appropriate only if the unequal treatment is "*rationally related to a legitimate state interest.*"
2. **Intermediate Scrutiny**: For more protected classes of people, such as gender, the unequal treatment of each gender by the law will be constitutionally appropriate only if it is "*substantially related to a sufficiently important governmental interest.*"
3 **Strict Scrutiny**: For the most protected classes of people, such as the racial classes of people, the unequal treatment of one race over another by the law will be Constitutionally appropriate only if it is "*suitably tailored* [or *necessary and involving the least restrictive means available*] to serve a *compelling state interest.*" This test is also used when governmental laws affect the fundamental Constitutional rights of individuals, such as free speech. The test determines whether the laws are appropriate or if they are overbroad and need modifications.

The Rational Basis Test in Action at the U.S. Supreme Court

Let's consider the Rational Basis Test in action on the issue of physician-assisted suicide. The United States Supreme Court, in

Washington v. Glucksberg, came to the conclusion that "the asserted 'right' to assistance in committing suicide is *not* a fundamental liberty interest protected by the due process clause," which would have required the law banning suicide to pass the most difficult scrutiny test in order to be deemed a valid and Constitutional law. The right to assisted suicide not being a fundamental liberty interest, the Constitution only requires that a state's "assisted suicide ban" be "rationally related to legitimate government interests," making it much easier for the ban to remain as a valid law.[7]

The court listed a number of state interests: the preservation of human life; the avoidance of serious public-health problems; protecting the integrity and ethics of the medical profession; and preventing the downward path to involuntary euthanasia.

The court noted that the downward path to euthanasia is a risk supported by evidence about euthanasia in the Netherlands. The evidence showed that in 1990 there were more than 1,000 cases of euthanasia that were completed *without* an explicit request and an additional 4,941 cases happened where physicians administered lethal morphine overdoses *without* the patients' explicit consent. Based on the legitimate government interests and the rational relationship of the law banning suicides to promote those interests, the law was and is not a violation of equal protection. Laws like these in other states that ban assisted suicide are, therefore, not unconstitutional.

The Spiritual Truth Scrutiny Tests

Like the legal tests, my tests for Spiritual Truth Scrutiny include three increasingly stronger sets of requirements for determining whether a spiritual or religious idea that applies to us passes scrutiny as being certainly true or not. The stronger tests can help us know if we have arrived at the higher degrees of certainty about the truth or not.

Knowing the requirements help us realize that we don't have to be satisfied with a merely more-likely-true-than-not standard in every aspect of the truth. Positions like, "God's reality is more likely true than not; therefore, I say He's real," or "I have no reason not to believe the Church is true," are not levels of certainty about the truth that we have to resign ourselves to. Higher certainties can be achieved.

This is a critically important point to understand. I'm not bashing personal testimony that's based on beliefs or faith. I'm not criticizing those who have the divine "gift to believe" (see D&C 46:14), which gives a person the divine conviction of the truth without needing a specific experience for it. But, through all of the explanations, descriptions, and illustrations that I have yet to elaborate on, I am encouraging people to diligently seek for, patiently await, and then obtain higher levels of certainty in the truthfulness of the "truths" they live by. This will have a great effect for good in their spiritual lives and a very good effect in their secular lives. It will aid them in many ways, including that of jury duty and deciding the future of accused people's lives and the potentially life-long consequences for the guilty ones.

In Spiritual Truth Scrutiny, the three tests that I've named the same as the constitutional tests are:

- Rational Basis Test
- Intermediate Scrutiny
- Strict Scrutiny

WHY THESE TESTS ARE RELEVANT TO EVERYDAY LIFE

Before we go into further detail about each test, we need to remember that the long-term goal of becoming acquainted with these tests (for purposes of this book) is to ultimately be able to roughly apply them to people accused of *sinful* conduct (not necessarily *criminal* conduct because the law is already well established in how to determine the certainty of beyond a reasonable doubt as to whether a person committed a crime or not).

As we roughly apply these tests to judging people, as opposed to only concepts of truth, we are enabled to "[j]udge not according to the appearance, but judge righteous judgment" (John 7:24). We will make fewer mistakes in convicting and condemning the innocent in our own minds and hearts. And, as a result, we will better understand and appreciate the Christlike role of a criminal defense lawyer who optimistically believes in the widespread, inherent goodness of humanity and individuals.

THE RATIONAL BASIS TEST

Under the Rational Basis Test, a religious or spiritual idea must meet two requirements or qualifications to give us a level of certainty that it is true. It must be (1) rational and it must be based on (2) a legitimate spiritual event (and just about any will do). The following chart summarizes the test and the resulting, general certainty in a broad way of speaking:

REQUIREMENTS FOR CERTAINTY	RESULTING GENERAL CERTAINTY
1. Rational	Belief—acceptance of an idea
2. Legitimate Spiritual Event (any will do)	

When we use this standard for becoming certain of truth, a lot of spiritual or religious ideas will pass as ones we can accept as true. That acceptance is a level of certainty. In other words, we can believe them. The spiritual or religious idea only has to be what we consider to be rational and be grounded in some spiritual event that we consider legitimate. The spiritual event does not even have to be our own. It can be one that we've only heard or read about. It can be one that a person, whom we don't know personally, experienced in some distant place or time. Basically, any spiritual event will do because, realistically, this test tends to be more subjective than objective since reasonable minds can differ markedly as to what is legitimate.

Let's put this test into practice to make it more understandable.

SIGNS INDICATING USE OF RATIONAL BASIS TEST

It Is Right for Me: One of the clear signs that a person is only using the Rational Basis Test (or perhaps even the lower standard of make-believe) in their "spiritual career"[8] is when they say that the religious or spiritual idea, or even a church, "must be right *for me*" and they mean it they way they said it. They say it not simply as an attempt to avoid conflict or hurt a relationship. They also may say, "You have to follow what works *for you*." These clearly subjective statements demonstrate, at best, the use of the lowest degrees of certainty for truth because what's right or works for you is only rationally something that must be true *for you* and not necessarily true for someone else. Usually, in the spiritual career context, what's right or works for you will have some basis in at least some distant or abstract spiritual experience to validate the thing as legitimately spiritual or religious. If there is no such spiritual basis whatsoever, then the idea or truth is merely philosophical, scientific, legal, academic, or political.

Having a Relationship with Christ: Another, more subtle use of the lower standards of truth in the spiritual career context is when someone says that what's really important is "having a relationship with Christ" or a "relationship with God." But how can these be criticized? Generally speaking, there's nothing wrong with them—it's highly important to have a relationship with Christ, who is our Lord, our God, and our King, and it's highly important to also have a relationship with God the Father and with the Holy Ghost. But what is, and what is not, a "relationship"? If we reject Them, then we don't really have a meaningful relationship with Them. A mutual or meaningful relationship with God on some level should be a part of all of our lives. More particularly, we need to have a *proper* relationship with God because even repeat sinners have a relationship with Christ—He has suffered and died for them. They may even believe that and love Him for it. That's a close relationship from their perspective, but not the proper, ideal one.

The proper, ideal relationship would be one where we *know* ("And this is life eternal, that they might *know* thee the only true God, and Jesus Christ, whom thou has sent" [John 17:3, emphasis added]), love, trust, always remember, rely on, and emulate Christ in order to be one with Him and the Father (recall Christ's prayers for this kind of a relationship: "And now Father, I pray unto thee for them . . . that I may be in them as thou, Father, art in me, that we may be one" [3 Nephi 19:23] that "they also may be one in us . . . that they may be made perfect in one" [John 17:21, 23]) *and* where He can also love, trust, and guide us to be one with Him and to do His work with Him. That's the mutual part of it. It should be a connection where we can always have His Spirit to be with us. It is a relationship of drawing close in reverence to the character and likeness and conduct of Christ, our Older Brother, and where we would worship and revere God the Father in awe as His literal spirit children and as His sincere followers. In short, we are to have an appropriate family-in-Heaven relationship with Them.

The accurate teachings of Christ's gospel as recorded in all of the scriptures and the precise religion He established and reestablished modernly through His prophets today are the only directions (coupled with those from the Holy Ghost and with grace through the Atonement of Christ) that can enable us to truly create an ideal and proper relationship with the Godhead, as I understand. God will best establish His part of the relationship as we sincerely try to follow those ways that He's provided. Then, through Christ's grace, we will have a *saved* relationship "after all we can do" (2 Nephi 25:23).

Generally speaking, though, the unspecified "having a relationship" position uses the lower to lowest degrees of certainty about truth when people claim that a proper relationship with Christ or the Father can be formed *without* seeking and practicing the actual *religion and church* Christ Himself organized. Likewise, people use these lower degrees of certainty when they claim to have a loose, informal friendship that doesn't recognize the relationship as Creator to the created, Father to son or daughter, and Leader to follower. People who take either of these positions frequently believe organized religion of any kind tends to take a person away from a relationship with Christ or with God the Father of our spirits. Admittedly, some organized religions and churches will have that negative effect, but certainly not Christ's own religion and church.

If there is a negative effect associated with Christ's own religion and Church, then it is the way *people* use and respond to His religion that creates the negative effect. But that's not the fault of Christ's teachings or organized church. In another way of looking at it, Christ's organized religion is like a hammer—it is a useful and essential tool for building a home, but it can also be used as a weapon to harm others. If used as a weapon, it's not the hammer's fault or the maker of the hammer's fault that it was used inappropriately. The user is at fault because the hammer was meant to build, not harm.

Those who have this type of conviction—that a mere friendship relationship with Christ or with God the Father is the only thing that matters in a person's spirituality—can deviate from Christ's official teachings yet still feel a connection as long as they are spiritual in a general Christian sense. Outside of that, they enjoy a mainly self-centered spiritual life, replete with their own personal rules *they* have engineered. They become laws unto themselves. In the most severe cases, "That which breaketh a law, and abideth not by law, but seeketh to become a law unto itself, and willeth to abide in sin, and altogether abideth in sin, cannot be sanctified by law, neither by mercy, justice, nor judgment. Therefore, they must remain filthy still" (D&C 88:35). In the average case of simply doing their own things, but not altogether abiding in sin, they can still consider their spirituality as a legitimate "relationship" with Christ or the Father. And they're right. They have a *legitimate* relationship with God. Heavenly Father is still their Father and Christ is their Savior, who died for them. That's a legitimate relationship between them.

As we explore other standards of truth or degrees of certainty, however, we'll see that a *legitimate* relationship with God is rivaled by more appropriate relationships with Deity. These could be described as *important* relationships with God and *compelling* relationships with God, named after the standards in the two higher scrutiny tests that we have yet to consider.

Why Low Degrees of Certainty in Our Personal Lives Can Be Harmful

And again, just so we stay on track, remember that being highly certain of truth in our spiritual lives is important because getting used to lower degrees of certainty (such as just doing "what's right for me" or having a loose, informal friendship relationship with Christ) can easily lead us into believing it is acceptable to make final judgments of others based on similarly low degrees of certainty. And when we are used to that, it spills over into our lives as jury members when we have to judge a person and we make mistakes about him or her with long-lasting effects on the one that we misjudged. The long-lasting effects from our mistaken judgments could even carry over into our own lives according to Christ's declaration, "For with what judgment ye judge, ye shall be judged" (Matthew 7:2).

The "Belief" from the Rational Basis Test Has at Least Two Varying Degrees

Going back to the Rational Basis Test itself, if we see that the spiritual or religious idea passes this test, then the resulting degree of certainty falls into the general category of "belief"—the acceptance of an idea. The confidence in your belief can come in at least two degrees of certainty: "reasonable, articulable suspicion" (RAS), and "probable cause" (PC).

Recall that RAS is when there is at least some degree of evidence that leads a reasonable person to *suspect* something is or is not true (or suspect that criminal activity is afoot) *and* that person can genuinely verbalize what the evidentiary basis is. And remember that "probable cause" is when there's enough evidence to lead a reasonable person to *believe* something is or is not true (or believe that a crime was committed by a specific individual). Thus, to achieve the "belief" level of certainty, there must be some minimum amount of fact or evidence to lead a reasonable person to suspect or believe something as being probably true.

A "Hunch" Is Not a Degree of Belief

The Rational Basis Test category does not include a hunch, even though a hunch is, by a loose interpretation of the phrase, a degree of certainty about the truth. A hunch lacks a minimum basis of fact or evidence to lead a *reasonable* person to suspect or believe one way or the other—as Professor Jaeger would say, such a belief (that is, a hunch) is not grounded in anything in the public, observable world and is nothing more than a profound delusion based on fantasy.[9]

Specific Examples of the Weakness of the Rational Basis Test's "Belief"

A couple more examples of this test may help demonstrate the low levels of certainty that it takes to pass it. So you can more easily relate, I will take from spiritual or religious examples. I don't mean to be unfairly critical or disrespectful in any way to any faith. Rather I hope these examples will serve as effective illustrations.

BIBLE TRANSLATIONS

Take the religious stance with the (1) "rational" (which is the first part of the Rational Basis Test analysis) and (2) "legitimate spiritual experience" (second part) analysis:

1. The current Bible translations are flawed because they omit the original name "Jehovah" and replace it with "Lord";
2. The Bible was received by direct revelation to prophets of God, whereas the translators who added "Lord" never claimed to have received direct revelation to do so.

Under this analysis, the idea of flawed Bible translations for all or most of our Bibles is rational, based on the legitimate spiritual experiences of ancient prophets (and the translators' supposed lack thereof); thus, the stance on the imperfect Bible translations is a truth according to the Rational Basis Test.

The trouble with the Rational Basis Test is that a contradictory outcome can occur, yet the contradiction passes as truth too. For example:

1. Because the original name "Jehovah" is sacred and we are commanded to not take His name "in vain" (*see* Exodus 20:7), it is proper to replace it with a substitute name;
2. Moses, the great prophet of God, received this commandment about keeping God's name sacred directly from God Himself.

Thus, the conclusion that our current Bibles are *not* flawed by the substitutions is a rational one. It is based on the legitimate spiritual experience of Moses and God's direction to him and the logically related method of living God's direction by avoiding the too frequent use of His name by way of a substitute name.

Because both positions contradict each other and can't both be absolutely right, which stance is actually true? Unfortunately, the

Rational Basis Test *can never* answer this question. If people are satisfied with only meeting the requirements of this test in order to believe in something (such as believing a person's sinfulness because the accusation is "rationally" related to a legitimate *sinful* event, rather than "spiritual" event), then they will always have beliefs in contradiction with others, including those who are similarly satisfied with their spiritual or religious ideas only passing this test. In short, they will never be able to agree.

Perhaps this explains why religion throughout history has caused so much strife and warfare—too many followers of the various sects and religions only *believe* their churches rather than make the effort to achieve higher levels of certainty such as *strong faith*, *knowledge*, or *perfect knowledge* in their churches. They mistakenly treat their contradictory spiritual or religious ideas as being completely true when the ideas only meet the requirements of being rational and based on a spiritual experience—the "belief" standards. Then the various believers fight each other about the contradictions. They act as if they are absolutely certain the others are wrong when they are actually only somewhat certain that their own beliefs are right. The history of the Protestant Reformation is a specific example of how so many churches could sprout up. Each of the many founders followed what was rational or even substantially convincing and not what was necessarily a compelling witness of what is actually true. They may have been right and inspired in a lot of areas, but they were also significantly wrong in others due to the inherent weakness of a lack of knowledge.

COINCIDENCES

Another example of a person using only this test to discover truth is when their religious or spiritual idea is supported by some circumstance that happens out of the ordinary—it appears that the circumstance was divinely caused. A clear example of the weakness inherent in this degree of certainty comes from the history of the Japanese nation.[10] Anciently, the Japanese people came to believe that their country was a divine nation. This belief developed from the fact that when the vast armies of Mongolian invaders came to destroy their nation, the armies were stopped *twice* on two totally separate occasions by enormous storms that suddenly arose. As a result, many Japanese people believed their nation and leader were divine. Their spiritual beliefs spilled over into their secular lives; they began conquering nearby nations to spread their nation's divinity throughout the world. Centuries later, however, many of the Japanese people totally lost their faith when their "divine" nation was decimated by two nuclear bombs from America. The events of Hiroshima and Nagasaki proved their particular beliefs false. The later proof, though, does not mean that their initial beliefs did not pass the Rational Basis Test—they had.

These examples show how the Rational Basis Test is open to wide interpretations and guessing. In the end, because the legitimate spiritual experience can be so distant, the test can unfortunately be passed by ideas that are wrong and merely rational in a subjective sense due to the fact that reasonable minds can differ. Rational concepts and spiritual events of *any* sort, without proper regard to their inherent reliability or unreliability, are very shaky foundations for establishing truth. In other words, mere belief is risky in governing one's spiritual or religious life.

APPLYING RATIONAL BASIS TEST TO JUDGING OTHERS

Consequently, applying only the Rational Basis Test to religion will lead to mistaken faith and strife. Applying a secularized version of the test to people and the wrongs they commit will also lead to similar outcomes. The secularized version is that (1) the accusations of wrongdoing must be "rationally" related to some form of "legitimate" evidence of a sinful event. Because of the inherent weaknesses of the Rational Basis Test, using the secularized version of it in our judgments of people accused of misconduct will inevitably lead us to wrong viewpoints and improper treatment of them. It, therefore, should not be used in the criminal context where so much is at stake: the deprivation of life, liberty, property, and the pursuit of happiness.

Notes

1. The evidentiary standards of truth: hunch, reasonable, articulable suspicion (RAS), probable cause (PC), preponderance of the evidence (PE), clear and convincing evidence (CCE), beyond a reasonable doubt (BARD), and absolute knowledge.
2. The spiritual standards of truth: desire to believe, cause to believe, belief, faith, strong faith, knowledge, and perfect knowledge.
3. Desire to believe/hunch, cause to believe/RAS, belief/PC, faith/PE, strong faith/CCE, knowledge/BARD, and perfect knowledge/absolute knowledge.
4. These methods may include, but are not limited to (1) prayer, (2) reading scriptures, (3) pondering their content, (4) applying the scriptural lessons, (5) attending church meetings, (6) living worthily by keeping all the commandments as best as you can, (7) repenting when making mistakes, (8) testifying of what you believe, have faith in, and/or know, (9) sharing Christ's Gospel with others, and (10) consistently living a Christlike life and doing good to others (especially to family)—by doing these actions, you are following the methods for discovering truth and growing closer to Christ in a proper relationship with Him, our Deity.
5. *Cleburne v. Cleburne Living Center*, Inc., 473 US 432 (1985). Emphasis and clarifications added.
6. *See FS Royster Guano Co. v. Virginia*, 253 US 412, 415 (1920).
7. *Washington v. Glucksberg*, 521 US 702 (1997), emphasis added.
8. "Spiritual career" comes from the ancient Hindu scripture, the Bhagavad-Gita, which states, "Without direct experience, one has to rely on theory and concepts; theorizing and make-believe have no place in one's spiritual career."
9. "Belief is grounded in something, unlike fantasy which isn't grounded in anything. If you can't point to something in the public, observable world, then we would say that that belief is not good enough. Ungrounded belief wipes out malice but establishes that the person is profoundly deluded." Professor Jaeger, Criminal Law, 2002.
10. See *Mankind's Search for God*, Watch Tower Bible and Tract Society of Pennsylvania (Watchtower Bible and Tract Society of New York, Inc. and International Bible Students Association, Brooklyn: New York, 1990), 197–203.

10

INTERMEDIATE SCRUTINY

Under the Intermediate Scrutiny Test, a religious or spiritual idea must meet two qualifications. It must be *substantially* convincing and be based on an *important* spiritual experience or experiences. The following chart summarizes the test and the resulting general certainty:

REQUIREMENT FOR CERTAINTY	RESULTING GENERAL CERTAINTY
1. Substantially Convincing	Faith—assurances in or evidence of unseen things being true
2. Important Spiritual Experience (personal and specific: most important)	

When we use this standard for determining truth, many spiritual or religious "truths" are excluded as being certainly true. They fail to pass Intermediate Scrutiny. Many spiritual or religious ideas, even though rational and true according to the first test, are not substantially convincing as being truth from God because they are not based on important spiritual experiences.

There is a degree of objectivity in this test; being substantially convincing is much more than merely meeting some individual's personal, subjective definition of what is rational and legitimate, like in the Rational Basis Test. It means being substantially convincing to more than just one person—usually much more than just one person. And it means the idea has an inherent quality of correctness—it not only intellectually seems right, but also feels right.

WHAT DOES IMPORTANCE MEAN FOR AN "IMPORTANT" SPIRITUAL EXPERIENCE?

Closeness to You: What is an *important* spiritual experience? I submit that the more closely the spiritual experience is tied to a reliable source that you have good reason to trust (such as a close family member's experience, close friend's, a trusted religious leader's) or the more personal the experience is to you (as in you experienced it yourself), the more important it is. When it comes to who experienced the spiritual event, it is *most* important if you personally experienced the spiritual event because then you are an eyewitness of the event and not relying on any hearsay.

Specificity: How specific the subject matter of the spiritual event is also adds to its importance in discovering truth. The nature of the event cannot be abstract so that someone could draw far too many speculative conclusions from it. Coincidental experiences are frequently too abstract to pass this test because too many speculative conclusions can be drawn from them that are often contradictory.

The Mongolian invaders of Japan, which we discussed in the previous chapter, are a good example. The fact that two separate storms stopped the invaders creates only the speculative conclusion that your nation and leader are divine—those points of truth do not clearly present themselves from those sets of facts. Such an event could simply mean that God wanted to protect people from unwarranted harm. Even that, though, is somewhat speculative. Nothing verified that God Himself sent the storms to stop the invaders. No prophet claiming authority to speak in His name declared it. No vision, revelation, or prophecy verified it. The storms could simply have been coincidences. Hence, the "important" experience must *specifically* relate to an *identifiable point of truth*. The specific relation between the experience and the truth so substantially convinces you (and potentially many others) of that point of truth (this relates only to when your spiritual experiences teach you about truth, rather than a spiritual experience that has a totally different purpose, such as to comfort you). Thus, the circumstances around the event make the event either more or less substantially convincing as one coming from God, and, therefore, more or less important.

THE "FAITH" FROM THE INTERMEDIATE SCRUTINY TEST HAS AT LEAST THREE VARYING DEGREES

When the spiritual or religious truths pass this test, the resulting degree of certainty is in the general category of faith. Of the evidentiary standards of truth, three can fall into this category: preponderance of the evidence (PE), clear and convincing evidence (CCE), and even the "knowledge" standard of proof beyond a reasonable doubt (BARD).

SPECIFIC EXAMPLES OF THE STRENGTH OF THE INTERMEDIATE SCRUTINY TEST'S "FAITH"

Vegetarianism: An example of a spiritual or religious idea that passes Intermediate Scrutiny would be as follows, as stated by a (hypothetical) religious person: (1) being vegetarian (not eating meat) is the proper way of a spiritual life because (2) a modern-day prophet, Ellen G. White, received this doctrine by revelation and I'm a member of the Seventh-day Adventist Church that she was a part of, and (3) I've tried it and felt better, and (4) secular knowledge proves its worth in extending life.

This example passes Intermediate Scrutiny because the idea is substantially convincing as true. It is based on a solid, important spiritual experience—revelation. The significant spiritual event here is associated with a modern-day person, not just some person in the distant past. The claim is also powerful—she claims to be a prophet receiving revelation directly from the Source of all truth. The experience is specific in that it precisely relates to the point of truth: vegetarianism. The other person involved, who is a hypothetical member of the church, has personally tried the doctrine and discovered for himself that it makes him feel better. Not only is the doctrine merely spiritual, but it is also supported by the secular, circumstantial evidence: people who live a vegetarian diet do actually live longer than others, generally speaking.[1]

All of these reasons make the spiritual or religious idea that vegetarianism is the right way of life substantially convincing. The idea passes Intermediate Scrutiny. However, this does not make us certain that the idea is necessarily truth. We are merely more certain than not that it is an absolute truth. We can confidently live the idea by faith, unless we gain actual knowledge that it is wrong. This point of truth about vegetarianism would have to pass the Strict Scrutiny Test in order to be firmly established with total certainty as an absolute truth.

APPLYING INTERMEDIATE SCRUTINY TO JUDGING OTHERS

When it comes to roughly applying this test to people accused of sin, the secularized version of Intermediate Scrutiny would require that the accusations of guilt be "substantially convincing" through being based on "important" indicators of sinfulness. To be most important, the indicators must be closely tied by facts to the person accused and be specific.

Note

1. This general fact is frequently noted in scientific literature and can be quickly found by a simple Internet search.

11

STRICT SCRUTINY

Under the Strict Scrutiny Test, a religious or spiritual idea must meet three qualifications. It must be based on *knowledge* from *a compelling witness* that comes from *no other source than God*:

REQUIREMENTS FOR CERTAINTY	RESULTING CERTAINTY
1. Knowledge is Necessary	Perfect Knowledge—perfectly knowing with absolute certainty in mind, heart, and spirit
2. Compelling Witness (of the kind that none is stronger)	
3. No Other Source than God	

When we use this standard for determining truth, truths that pass Intermediate Scrutiny can fail this test as being certainly false ideas. The spiritual or religious truth must be supported by knowledge that is grounded in a compelling witness. The compelling witness must have no other source than God and the witness must be of the kind that none is stronger. The compelling witness can only be what you personally have experienced, making you an eyewitness rather than anything less. The compelling witness must be of a magnitude and quality that you actually know it came from God as opposed to coming from yourself, mankind, or Satan.

"No Other Source than God" Means the Holy Ghost Must Be Present

To be certain the witness came from God, the undeniable influence of the Holy Ghost must, at some point, be present to validate the compelling witness. These compelling witnesses could come in the form of a vision, revelation, miracle, healing, clear answer to prayer, or other strong spiritual witness. Without the powerful or divine influence of the Holy Ghost, though, the compelling witness could very well have come from the adversary or some other source. In other words, there will be room to doubt the validity of the strong witness and the resulting knowledge.

The "Perfect Knowledge" from Strict Scrutiny Has Only One Degree of Certainty: 100%

This perfect knowledge is the highest degree of certainty. Of the standards of truth that can fall into this category, there is only one: absolute knowledge. This knowledge is probably best described in the scriptures as "perfect knowledge," not just "knowledge" (see, for example, the difference between the two in 2 Nephi 9:13—"all men become . . . immortal, and they are living souls, having a perfect knowledge like unto us in the flesh, save it be that our knowledge shall be perfect"). I submit that when you gain absolute or perfect knowledge of something, you also know with complete certainty that the knowledge came from God instead of simply from your own senses, mind, experiences, or Satan. Sources other than God can only bring you the witness of experiential knowledge; even human, experiential knowledge cannot rival the witness that comes from God. Remember, "What greater witness can you have than from God?" (D&C 6:23). With perfect knowledge, you also possess a second knowledge that independently verifies the truthfulness of the compelling witness you receive.

Specific Examples of the Absoluteness of the Strict Scrutiny Test's "Perfect Knowledge"

An example of a spiritual or religious idea passing Strict Scrutiny is one that I can give you from one of my own experiences. The idea of a Supreme Being or God passes strict scrutiny when you can say (1) I *know* from *personal experience* (in essence, as an eyewitness) that a Supreme Being of some sort exists; (2) this knowledge comes from both my mind and heart when I experienced His direct influence—I felt Him powerfully as His influence forcefully pierced my own spirit's heart and ideas, independent from my own, simultaneously entered my mind and verified it was from Him; and (3) there was no other source for this than the Supreme Being (or God) because the powerful, piercing sensation caused me feelings of the ultimate good: joy, love, and peace of a magnitude, intensity, and purity that I'd never felt before.

These feelings came without me doing anything physically significant to generate them on my own. There was no adrenalin rush or euphoria from physical activity or strict mental exertion to force it to occur. It happened during the minimal activity of listening to a speaker talk about religious matters, which were directly related to the spiritual experience and the points of truth gleaned from the experience. The speaker's words were not just abstract and arbitrary matters unrelated to the spiritual experience. The supernal feelings I had are inherently good, even from a secular point of view. The independent, uplifting thoughts also verified the reality that this was from the Supreme Being and not from man (such as drugs or rousing social group activity), my own body (adrenalin or chemical euphoria), or the father of all lies, Satan.

Objective Indications of Receiving Perfect Knowledge

Changed Lifestyle: With few exceptions, every person who has experienced a compelling witness will voluntarily change his or her lifestyle to be in conformity with the witness. This is not to say that every person who has significantly changed his or her life on account of some spiritual experience must have experienced a compelling witness; that is a logical fallacy. People often change their lives for less. But, of those who do change their lifestyles, you will find that the vast majority of those experiencing a compelling witness from God will be among them. They will almost inevitably put their lives in voluntary harmony with their experience. For example, but not limited to these examples, they will live very good lives, share their experience(s) to help others have better lives and understand the truth more fully, want to bless the whole human race instead of only themselves and their family, and will be sincerely devoted to loving God and others. Malice will be wiped out of their hearts; importantly, though, much of their views, behavior, habits, and actions will be down to earth and evidence no degree of being "profoundly deluded" by any reasonable standard.

This significant change that happens in the person's life is visible, even though some may attribute the change to a different source or cause. What's significant is that the public, observable world can see the visible effects of the divine witness, although they are free to speculate and doubt the cause of the change and the genuineness of it just as judges and juries can do toward an eye-witness's testimony in court.

Consistency with Others: Furthermore, the person who experienced the compelling witness will specially relate to others who have claimed to have received the same witness. The descriptions are highly consistent with each other. Consider Joseph Smith's experience while reading James 1:5, which included two witnesses—one to his heart and the other to his mind. He said:

> Never did any passage of scripture come with more *power to the heart* of man than this did at this time to mine. It seemed to *enter with great force* into every feeling of my heart. I *reflected on it again and again, knowing* that if any person needed wisdom from God, I did. Joseph History 1:12. (Emphasis added)

Consider also other consistent scriptures about the compelling witness of the Holy Ghost:

> Helaman 5:30—"And it came to pass when they heard this voice, and beheld that it was not a voice of thunder, neither was it a voice of a great tumultuous noise, but behold, it was a still voice of perfect mildness, as if it had been a whisper, and *it did pierce even to the very soul.*" (Emphasis added)

3 Nephi 11:3—"And it came to pass . . . they heard a voice as if it came out of heaven . . . and notwithstanding it being a small voice *it did pierce them that did hear to the center*, insomuch that there was no part of their frame that it did not cause to quake; yea, *it did pierce them to the very soul*, and *did cause their hearts to burn*." (Emphasis added)

Romans 8:16—"The Spirit itself beareth witness *with our spirit*, that we are the children of God." (Emphasis added)

The compelling witness, therefore, is again grounded in something observable—in the *consistency* of the witnesses that manifest themselves in the descriptions of what happened and the observable lifestyles and consistent claims of others that experienced them.

Just as emotions themselves are not observable, but the effects of them are, the same is true for compelling witnesses and the lifestyles that emerge. My criminal law professor's criticism has no bearing whatsoever when it comes to witnesses on the level of strict scrutiny:

"Belief is grounded in something, unlike fantasy, which isn't grounded in anything. If you can't point to something in the public, observable world, then we would say that that belief is not good enough. Ungrounded belief wipes out malice but establishes that the person is profoundly deluded."

Anyone who has not experienced this kind of spiritual event or witness to any degree, however, will certainly be able to have reasonable doubts about its validity for that very reason—they have not experienced it themselves. They were not eyewitnesses; thus, they cannot *know perfectly* if it is true. Hence, there is room for doubt.

HOW MUCH CERTAINTY DOES YOUR PERFECT KNOWLEDGE BRING TO OTHERS?

If we take the reality of a Supreme Being and my experience for an example, people can only posses a *belief*, which can either be the lower degree of belief, *reasonable, articulable suspicion (RAS)*, or perhaps even the higher degree of belief, which is *probable cause (PC)* that a Supreme Being is real, based on my claims of a compelling witness and absolute knowledge. They can believe it as true based on my legitimate, spiritual experience that is rationally-related to the spiritual idea of "God." They can also choose to disbelieve it as being legitimate or rational because reasonable minds can differ and yet still be rational.

Counterfeits

There is one last issue I want to address in this part of the book regarding the Spirit of God, counterfeits, and the knowledge or reasonable conclusions drawn from counterfeits.

I have a friend who became atheist because of an ability he mastered in replicating what he thought the Spirit of God felt like. While driving in his car one day and listening to a pop culture song, he heard a woman hit a very high note. When she hit this high note, my friend also felt a rush of adrenalin. That rush is what he always associated with the Spirit. He began to mentally exert his will enough to recreate the rush. He succeeded. Over time, he could generate that same rush within himself whenever he wanted. He concluded from reason that if he was able to physically recreate the sensation of what he thought the Spirit feels like, then there must be no God—that God's "Spirit" was nothing more than a self-engineered, human sensation.

From the perspective of the Rational Basis Test, his pseudo-spiritual event and conclusion are rational, or at least they give reasonable doubt in the reality of God's Spirit being divine instead of carnal.

Reasonable minds, however, can differ on his conclusion. Reason could also say that just because an expert counterfeiter can make a realistic-looking, counterfeit one-hundred dollar bill, that does not mean real one-hundred dollar bills are all fake. My friend is only using the Rational Basis Test to determine the truth of the matter about God's existence or non-existence because his conclusion is not substantially convincing (although it is based on a personal experience) because his logical conclusion can be so easily contradicted by the analogy to the expert counterfeiter.

The legitimacy of my friend's "spiritual" event is also questionable because it came at an arbitrary time, and it does not follow the scriptural pattern of what the Spirit of God can be like when He's teaching truth—His influence is not always simply a feeling in your heart or a rush of adrenalin as my friend considered it *every time.* (See Galatians 5:22–23: "But the fruit of the Spirit is love, joy, peace, longsuffering, gentleness, goodness, faith, Meekness, [and] temperance." Notice the scripture does not say "the fruit of the Spirit is *always* love, joy, peace." Without the word "always," the meaning of "is" becomes "includes" and does not limit the fruit only to those listed.)

There are different manifestations at different times. The Spirit's influence can come both to your heart *and* to your mind: "[V]erily, verily, I say unto you, that assuredly as the Lord liveth, who is your God and your Redeemer, even so surely shall you receive a *knowledge* of whatsoever things you shall ask *in faith*, with an honest heart, *believing* that you shall receive a knowledge. . . . Yea, behold, I will tell you in your mind and in your heart, by the Holy Ghost, which shall come upon you and which shall dwell in your heart. Now, behold, this is the spirit of revelation" (D&C 8:1–3, emphasis added), and in "the mouth of two or three witnesses [such as the mind and heart] shall every word [including God's doctrines] be established" (2 Corinthians 13:1).

There can be thoughts, independent from your own, that will verify the authenticity of the God-sent feelings and experiences. The thoughts that are not of your own making can teach you the truth of the matter you're questioning, and, thereby, give you knowledge. I know this from my own experiences. And I also know that this knowledge is even more certain than knowledge gained by experience—it rivals knowledge in practice.

Thus, my friend's belief in atheism passes, perhaps, the lowest standard of belief: reasonable, articulable suspicion. He has a reasonable and articulable suspicion that there is no God based on the "spiritual" event he had while driving and based on the repeated instances of recreating that sensation on demand.

If my friend were to apply a more stringent standard of spiritual scrutiny, then he would at least arrive at the conclusion that he does not have enough genuine witnesses either way to establish with any high degree of certainty whether God exists or not. Then, because he personally does not have enough genuine witnesses, he could then rely on the witness of other people who claim to have received those witnesses in order for him to at least *believe* there is a God.

Conversely, my friend could choose to believe atheists who claim to have a witness in the form of genuine evidence (not just rational arguments) in the non-existence of God.

At some point, however, in both examples, he needs to have a stronger witness for himself or he will simply be relying on hear-say—what other people hear and say—which provides only lower degrees of certainty. No one should be satisfied with those degrees of certainty fully governing their spiritual careers.

APPLYING STRICT SCRUTINY TO JUDGING OTHERS

As applied to the long-term goal of judging others properly, the version of this secular scrutiny test would be requiring "knowledge" that the person committed sin, which would be gained from "compelling" witnesses of the guilt, and that there would have to be no other source for that knowledge than God. If you could use this, then you would be able to view an individual as God views him or her. You would have a correct understanding of accountability and a complete comprehension of the manner in which the Atonement operates in that person's life.

If, as you apply these standards, you refuse to think negatively of a person until and if this test is met, then you would have an optimistic view of that person and be able to defend him without a poor attitude hampering your ability to provide a fair and zealous defense.

If, however, you knew a person was guilty, and that knowledge came from God, then you would likely also know God's aspirations for that individual in regards to changing. With that knowledge, you would defend that child of God by giving him the best chance at becoming the person who God would want him to become. Usually, the best chance for that is not simply incarceration—it's getting that person the help he needs to overcome his spiritual sickness. That help is usually from programs designed for the purpose of rehabilitation.

SUMMARY OF THE DEGREES OF CERTAINTY AND SCRUTINY TESTS

With all this being said, the following chart consolidates all of the prior information regarding the varying and roughly parallel degrees of certainty together with the scrutiny requirements for achieving the differing degrees of spiritual certainty about truth. I've arrived at each of these differing degrees of certainty for various truths based on a number of experiences that I've had. I have experienced each one and that's why I distinguish, for example, between faith and strong faith and knowledge and perfect knowledge:

Consolidated Chart: Degrees of Certainty, Standards of Truth, and Spiritual Truth Scrutiny

Standards of Evidence and Degrees of Certainty %	Source	Standards of Truth or Degrees of Spiritual Certainty	Requirements for Spiritual Degree Certainty	Resulting Spiritual Certainty (Generally)
Hunch—0%	Man alone can attain	Desire to Believe	Imagination, Speculation, Theory, Concepts, Conjecture	Make Believe: engineering your own ideas
Reasonable, Articulable Suspicion—25%	Man alone can attain	Cause to Believe	Rational Basis Test: (1) Rational, (2) Legitimate "Spiritual" Event	Belief: acceptance of an idea
Probable Cause—40%	Man alone can attain	Belief		

Civil Standards				
Preponderance of the Evidence—51%	Man alone can attain	Faith	Intermediate Scrutiny: (1)Substantially Convincing, (2)Important Spiritual Experience	FAITH: assurances in or evidence of unseen things being true
Clear and Convincing Evidence—70%	Man alone can attain	Strong Faith		
Criminal Standard				
Beyond a Reasonable Doubt—95%	Man alone can attain	Knowledge/To be sure		
Absolute Knowledge—100%	Only God-given	Perfect Knowledge Or Knowing of a surety by signs from Heaven	Strict Scrutiny: (1) Knowledge is Necessary, (2) Compelling Spiritual Witness (of the kind that none is stronger), (3) No Other Source than God	PERFECT KNOWLEDGE: perfectly knowing with absolute certainty in mind, heart, and spirit

12

INTELLECTUAL CERTAINTY: KNOWLEDGE BY EXTENSION AND FAILURE TO STATE A CLAIM UPON WHICH TRUE RELIGION CAN BE FOUNDED

KNOWLEDGE BY EXTENSION

Another degree of certainty is knowledge by extension. If, for example, you received a compelling witness from God that gives you absolute knowledge that the historical "Jesus Christ" was and is true and divine, then you could know by extension that the separate, specific teachings of His Gospel are also true, universally applicable, and from the Divine Source. This is predominantly an intellectual exercise in making appropriate connections.

Knowledge by extension is not as certain as actual knowledge because there can be errors in making the extensions. It is akin to "knowledge in theory" as Professor Flint referenced. These errors can result from logical fallacies, misinterpretations, inaccurate recordings, or even from your own sincere hopes, desires, and wishes. It can also come from make-believe.

For example, when discussing the religious idea of vegetarianism in a prior chapter, we saw how it can pass Intermediate Scrutiny. Knowledge by extension, however, can show that it fails Strict Scrutiny. A person who absolutely knows for themselves that the Bible is true, along with its separate teachings, can point to the scripture in 1 Timothy 4:1, 3 for knowledge by extension on the matter that says, "Now the Spirit speaketh expressly, that in the latter times some shall depart from the faith, giving heed to . . . doctrines of devils [which doctrines include] . . . commanding to abstain from meats, which God hath created to be received with thanksgiving of them which believe and know the truth." Thus, this person can know by extension that vegetarianism (not eating animal meat) is (perhaps) a doctrine of the devil.

The reason I say "perhaps" is because this knowledge by extension is still open to interpretation. Not every person knowing that the Bible and its separate teachings are true agrees on what this scripture is truly teaching. Some see "meat" as simply a word for "food," and there is a scriptural translation basis for this (Genesis 1:29: "And God said, Behold, I have given you every *herb* bearing seed, which is upon the face of all the earth, and every *tree*, in the which is the *fruit* of a tree yielding seed; to you it shall be for *meat."* See also the English Standard Version translation of the two scriptures: 1 Timothy 4:1, 3: "Now the Spirit expressly says that in later times some will depart from the faith by devoting themselves to deceitful spirits and teachings of demons . . . who . . . require abstinence from foods"; and Genesis 1:29: "And God said, Behold, I have given you every plant yielding seed that is on the face of all the earth, and every tree with seed in its fruit. You shall have them for food."). So, we see a weakness in knowledge by extension that comes, of necessity, from reasonable interpretations that can contradict each other.

Even with the inherent weaknesses of it, knowledge by extension can still yield a very high degree of certainty and is much safer and more valuable than *mere* beliefs since the extension is so closely tied to actual knowledge. In this way, there is a stronger basis for the acceptance of an idea being true that is beyond simply reason, hope, optimism, and some legitimate spiritual experience.

In many, if not most cases, knowledge by extension is only in the category of *strong faith* (which general category also includes "knowledge"), rather than *perfect knowledge*, since it is not knowledge gained directly from God or even by your own experiences. It can, therefore, be in the same degree of certainty within the evidentiary standards as is clear and convincing evidence (CCE) or beyond a reasonable doubt (BARD). It could, however, only be in the lower categories of certainty if the extension relies too much on rational interpretations, sincere hopes, wishes, or desires.

Applying this spiritual exercise to secular decisions, a member of a jury is permitted to extend the knowledge or proof received in court on certain issues to the ultimate question of whether the defendant is guilty. This helps him or her arrive at the needed degree of certainty, that is, beyond a reasonable doubt, to convict a person of a crime. The key is being sure that (1) the other issues have been proven with *knowledge* and (2) that they are sufficiently related to the ultimate issue before trying to extend that knowledge reliably.

FAILURE TO STATE A CLAIM UPON WHICH TRUE RELIGION MUST BE GROUNDED

There is another intellectual exercise that can bring a level of spiritual certainty about truth. It is based on a process of elimination. I've drawn a parallel between this process of elimination and a process of elimination that courts of law use. Courts can eliminate civil lawsuits from the outset when they fail to state a claim, or set out grounds, sufficient for a court to grant relief. Similarly, you can relate this to religions, churches, or forms of spirituality that fail to state or set out a spiritual basis that is sufficient for a true religion (or a true church or true form of spirituality) to be grounded upon. Let me elaborate.

Law: In a civil court of law (not a criminal court of law), the plaintiff must assert a sufficient claim in order for him to obtain relief. Initially, the court will *assume* that all of the plaintiff's claims are facts and are *true*. Even after the court assumes all of the assertions are true, if the plaintiff still has not asserted sufficient claims forming a basis for relief, then all of his claims will be dismissed and no longer considered—no longer tried to see if they are in fact true.[1] Further examination is unnecessary because even if all the claims and assertions were true, they do not amount to any legally material (or significant) truth. In these cases, legally material truth is only that which would allow some sort of financial gain/recovery or court order against the alleged wrongdoer.

The example of the tornado. To illustrate, if a plaintiff claims that he was injured and his car was destroyed in a tornado, the court would first presume that his claims are true: (1) that he was truly injured; (2) that he owned a car; (3) that there was a tornado; (4) that his car was destroyed by it; and (5) that his personal injuries resulted from the tornado. Even if all of his claims were true, however, the plaintiff still has not asserted sufficient claims upon which relief can be granted because tornados cannot be sued to provide relief. Thus, the plaintiff failed to state a claim upon which relief can be granted.

If, however, the plaintiff had claimed that the *government* failed to warn him of the tornado that injured him, then the court would follow the same process: first, assume that the government truly did fail to warn him of the impending tornado and assume that everything else happened as he claims. The second part of the process is to realize that this new claim would only be sufficient if the government, in fact, had a legal duty to warn him of the tornado in those circumstances. Does the government have that duty? If yes, then the case can be tried to see if the government actually failed and if it would have to pay him for his injuries and property damage. If, however, there were no legal duty, then the plaintiff would have again failed to state a claim upon which relief can be granted. Thus, no one would be responsible for making up for the injuries he experienced from the tornado.

Religion: In finding true religion, a true church, or true spirituality by a process of elimination (rather than by relying on knowledge by extension or on finding it based on certainty of truth gained directly from personal, spiritual experiences with the Source and Author of Truth), the situation is the same. Like the court, a person can first consider all the religious claims of a particular religion as being true.

If, even after assuming a religion's claims as all true, the religion still has not even claimed enough to be true, then that religion should not be considered any longer for purposes of discovering the truth. It should not even be further tested to see if its claims are in fact true. It has already failed. The person seeking for true religion could then move on to the next religion and consider its claims without first worrying whether the previous religion is actually true. As previously noted, this is also a predominantly intellectual exercise that can bring a level of certainty about truth. But it is not foolproof.

Errors can easily be made. Remember, reason is shaky ground to rely on for your testimony.

Based on what I believe is reasonable, true religion must have at least three claims. The absence of any one will constitute a failure to state a claim upon which true religion must be grounded: (1) absolute, sufficiently complete, and exclusive truthfulness; (2) teachings about a Supreme Being; and (3) origins in that Supreme Being. When these three claims are present, then the religion can be further examined to determine if its claims are true. If they are not present, then further examination is unnecessary.

APPLYING FAILURE-TO-STATE-A-CLAIM TO A HYPOTHETICAL EXAMPLE

To illustrate the utility of this exercise, a hypothetical example could be the ACME religion (A Corrupt Modernly Engineered religion). ACME religion's complete code of beliefs is as follows:

- Humans are the greatest of all animals
- Humans have potential
- Humans can reach their greatest potential through deep thought, serious reflection, and careful contemplation
- Each human should not rely on any other for achieving their individual potential
- Every person should spend a considerable amount of time every day in search of their true and greatest potential
- Once a week, people of this religion should gather together to speak of their progress toward their greatest potential
- They should worship those who have gone before and have reached their greatest potential through these methods

Let's examine the ACME religion by seeing if it has all three of the claims:

Claims to Be True: Note that in the ACME religion there is not a single claim of being absolutely, exclusively, or completely true in the areas that matter. This is one of the easiest indicators for finding a man-made religion instead of a God-made religion. Lacking a claim to be true indicates that the particular religion has failed to state a claim upon which true religion must be grounded.

If it is in fact the true religion or the true mode of spirituality, then it will claim it. The reason why it must make this claim is to avoid misleading people. Deception comes from lack of the claim because if it is in fact true, but does not claim itself to be true, then it will lead followers to believe that it is proper to *assume* the religion must be true even if it does not claim itself to be true.

As demonstrated in earlier chapters, an assumption as to what is true is nothing more than a desire to believe, a hunch, make-believe, or conjecture. These are unacceptable degrees of certainty. They fail to meet even the Rational Basis Test. An assumption of this kind leads to a form of blind obedience—blind because there is no acceptable degree of certainty. Thus, taking every claim of the ACME religion as true still would not produce a religion that is actually true because a true religion will claim that it is true to avoid the antithesis of truth: falsehoods, deceptions, misleading implications, and blind obedience. All ACME religion creates is a great philosophical and perhaps somewhat spiritual way of life.

What about factions? A number of major world religions have sufficient claims because they declare to be exclusively and completely true in a sufficient way. However, the major religions that claim to be exclusively true from other religions, but which are factionalized within themselves will again face this failure-to-state-a-claim problem because truth cannot contradict itself and still be true. It is a logical fallacy. Any material contradiction between factions is a clear indication of falsehood existing in at least one of the schisms.

In a factionalized religion claiming to be uniquely and completely true, each faction of that religion will be distinguished by distinctive teachings that must contradict in some way the teachings of another faction. At a minimum, one faction will have to imply that it is more complete with additional truth than another faction. Otherwise, there would be no factions—no differences and no distinctions between them that would distinguish them one from another.

Thus, if a particular religion claims to be uniquely true from other religions but has factions within it, then a person must take the next step of finding the true faction by the same process of elimination. The correct faction must claim to teach "the truth, the whole truth, and nothing but the truth" to properly state a claim upon which true religion must be grounded.

When we look at the Western and Near Eastern world religions that claim to be distinctively true, we find, for example, Judaism, Christianity, and Islam. Each religion claims to be exclusively and completely true, but each major religion is broken up into factions.

Some of Judaism's major, modern factions include Hassidic Jews, Orthodox Jews, Conservative Jews, Reconstructionist Jews, and Reform Jews.

Some of Christianity's major, modern factions include the Catholic, Protestant, Non-denominationalist, and Restorationist churches.

Some of Islam's major factions do and have included the Sunni, Shia, and Sufis.

In order for each faction to state a claim upon which true religion must be grounded, the factions need to also claim exclusive and complete truthfulness (and, at most, acknowledge that the other factions have truth, but not all of it). Otherwise, the faction is merely promoting a religious lifestyle that doesn't even claim to be objectively correct. It is only promoting a subjective, make-believe, engineered form of ordered spirituality that you can pick and choose for yourself. In these types of cases, the faction can only be a man-made religious schism and not a God-made religious division. Such a group is only meant to accommodate people who want their own religious preferences satisfied. Such a faction is not meant to satisfy people who want their religious preferences to conform to God's absolutely true preferences for His religion.

The ACME religion above does the same things that a man-made faction does. It only offers a subjectively correct spirituality because it makes no direct claims of objective truthfulness for its code of beliefs. In other words, the ACME religion only promotes the make-believe style of weakly spiritual thought that resembles self-chosen spirituality more than a God-driven religion. And, for some people, this is acceptable. That's how they want to live and they don't want to live anything more. Other people demand more of a religion and will only be satisfied by God's standards, not somebody else's opinions.

Claims of God: Another reason that ACME religion fails to state a claim upon which true religion must be grounded is its failure to teach anything about the Divine. Instead, it worships humanity. True religion and true spirituality must incorporate a belief in a Supreme Being to be distinct from philosophy, academics, science, law, or politics. It must not make earthly humanity the Supreme Being. Here, ACME religion is nothing more than philosophy. It may be an uplifting philosophy that helps a person or people achieve a level of goodness or spirituality ("spirituality" in the broad sense of the word) during this life, but it is not suited to do anything more than that, such as help lead them toward the full life God Himself lives.

Claims to Come from God: Another reason ACME religion fails to state a claim upon which true religion must be grounded is that it never claims to have origins with or in the Supreme Being. It never claims to have received its distinct tenets from a divine source. It's silent on the subject. Thus, ACME religion does not produce true religion or true spirituality that comes from God. It could just as well be a counterfeit of God's religion if it does not say anything one way or the other about where it comes from. Without such a claim, the ACME religion can easily produce confusion from misleading implications, deception, falsehoods, and blind obedience, as previously discussed.

Religions Not Failing to State Proper Claims: True religion is objectively true and not controlled by the subjective wishes of its participants. True religion and true spirituality is meant to bring its adherents closer to God in an appropriate relationship with Him. "Appropriateness" is from His perspective and measured by His standards; in other words, His preferences are what matter when it comes to an appropriate relationship. This relationship is not formed solely by the good-intended, intellectual efforts of the participants who rely on the shaky ground of reason to establish their beliefs. The relationship of unity comes from following God's directions and from receiving Christ's grace. True religion is established and maintained by God Himself in which people participate. Otherwise, it is a mankind religion in which "God" participates.

The Roman Catholic Church, The Church of Jesus Christ of

Latter-day Saints, and the Seventh-day Adventist Church are all examples of factions within the Christian faith that all state claims upon which true religion must be grounded. They each claim (1) to be exclusively, absolutely, and completely true from the others, (2) they teach about the Divine, and (3) they each claim to have originated from God Himself through Divine intervention to either ancient apostles or to modern-day prophets.

Specifically, when it comes to claims about God, originating from God, and being exclusively true, the Roman Catholic Church claims to have an unbroken line of priesthood authority from the Lord God Jesus Christ to the ancient Apostles and then to the modern-day popes.[2] The Church of Jesus Christ of Latter-day Saints claims to have its origins directly from God the Father and the Lord God Jesus Christ, who restored the ancient Gospel that was corrupted, and it also claims to be led by modern-day prophets, who receive direction from Them.[3] The Seventh-day Adventist Church claims to have received important knowledge of the truth through Ellen G. White, a woman claimed to be a modern-day prophet that received revelations and inspiration directly from God and the spirit of prophecy that He gave her.[4]

All of these claims combined together in each example are sufficient for being claims upon which true religion must be grounded. After narrowing down the Western Christian religions to at least those that make proper claims, we come to the next step: to determine which faith, if any, is in fact true—Catholics, Mormons, or Adventists (for example)? Which claims are the objectively correct ones? If we discover none are objectively true through the higher scrutiny tests, then we move onto Judaism and its factions, Islam and its factions, and the Eastern religions and their factions. The process continues until, with divine intervention, we can arrive at God's truth and know it with a high degree of certainty.

In contrast, with the example of the ACME religion, we do not even have to proceed to the next step of examining whether its codes of beliefs are actually true because its own claims, even if all taken as true, do not amount to anything more than man-made philosophy about a potentially "good" way of life.

It's important to keep in mind that "good" in modern

terminology is such a low standard of excellence. A "good" way of life is nearly meaningless because settling for such a low standard of excellence can never reach the ideal, such as the ideals of the best good and the absolute truth. The higher standards of truth, such as Intermediate and Strict Scrutiny, help us reach the higher goods and absolute truths. They help us avoid doctrines and concepts that stem only from imagination and make-believe.

Notes

1. A lower court stated this rule well after citing many other court decisions: "Finally, Federal Rule of Civil Procedure 12(b)(6) provides that a district court should dismiss a complaint for failure to state a claim upon which relief can be granted when it is clear that no relief could result under any facts consistent with the complaint's allegations. Thus, in evaluating defendants' Motion, the Court will assume the truth of all of the factual allegations set forth in plaintiffs Complaint and will construe the complaint liberally in favor of the plaintiff." *Collins v. Department of Interior*, 468 F. Supp. 2d 113 (U.S. District Court of Columbia 2006).
2. "[T]he Catholic priesthood has the indisputable right to trace its origin . . . to the Divine Founder of the Church." Catholic Encyclopedia, "Priesthood," http://www.newadvent.org/cathen/12409a.htm, as of July 21, 2010.
3. Joseph Smith, who claims that Christ restored His original church through him, alleges that before he did "so great were the confusion and strife among the different denominations, that it was impossible for a person young as I was . . . to come to any certain conclusion who was right and who was wrong. . . . At length I came to the conclusion that I must . . . ask of God. . . . [E]xerting all my powers to call upon God . . . I saw a pillar of light exactly over my head, above the brightness of the sun. . . . When the light rested upon me I saw two Personages, whose brightness and glory defy all description, standing above me in the air. One of them spake unto me, calling me by name and said, pointing to the other—This is My Beloved

Son. Hear Him! . . . I asked the Personages . . . which of all the sects was right. . . . I was answered that I must join none of them, for they were all wrong. . . . While . . . calling upon the Lord [years later], a messenger from heaven descended in a cloud of light, and having laid his hands upon us [Joseph and Oliver Cowdery], he ordained us, saying: Upon you my fellow servants, in the name of Messiah, I confer the Priesthood. . . . The messenger who visited us on this occasion . . . was . . . John the Baptist in the New Testament, and . . . he acted under the direction of Peter, James and John" (Joseph Smith History 1:7–72). Once The Church of Jesus Christ was restored, Joseph recorded the Lord's alleged words about ongoing revelation as follows, "I, the Lord, knowing the calamity which should come upon the inhabitants of the earth, called upon my servant Joseph Smith, Jun., and spake unto him from heaven. . . . And inasmuch as [my servants] were humble they might be . . . blessed from on high, and receive knowledge from time to time" (D&C 1:17, 28.)

4. The official website of the Seventh-Day Adventist Church states about the background setting for the actual organization, "Religious freedom came to mean . . . a right to read the Scripture for oneself and come to conclusions not bound by creedal presuppositions. The 'present truth' perspective assumed that new insights would arise as Seventh-day Adventists continued to study the Scriptures. The prophetic guidance of Ellen White within the movement solidified this perspective of social, organizational, and theological freedom. . . . The denomination was officially organized on May 21, 1863, when the movement included some 125 churches and 3,500 members." See http://www.adventist.org//world-church/facts-and-figures/history/index.html, as of July 21, 2010. The website continues, "We, the delegates to the 2010 General Conference Session in Atlanta, Georgia, acknowledge with gratitude the continuing contribution to the Seventh-day Adventist Church found in the writings and ministry of Ellen G. White. We are witnesses to how the Church has been blessed and guided by God through the inspired counsel of His messenger." See Resolution on the Spirit of Prophecy, http://www.adventist.org/beliefs/other-documents/spirit-of-prophecy.html, as of July 21, 2010.

13

PERSONAL PREFERENCES: THE BENEFITS OF STRICT SCRUTINY

Strict Scrutiny is my favorite test for determining critically important spiritual truths. The reality of God is one example. Which church, or God's form of spirituality, is another. Ideally, each person should fervently seek for his or her convictions in various truths from God to pass this test.

BENEFITS

Eliminate Doubt and Help Others: When some convictions in certain truths do pass, then their "spiritual careers"[1] become much more satisfactory and beneficial—these convictions eliminate sincere and reasonable doubts in some areas, and these people are then enabled to better help others who may be struggling with their own legitimate doubts in those areas.

Optimistic Presumptions: The other important benefit is that as we refuse to be satisfied by anything less than high degrees of certainty in areas of truth, this attitude will spill over into our personal lives and we will similarly only be satisfied with achieving higher degrees of certainty in matters of judging others. Without that certainty, we can optimistically believe in the inherent goodness of each person and be less quick to assume that they are 100 percent accountable for any wrong they may have done.

Correct Faith: As applied to our spiritual lives, another significant reason why we should each have absolute knowledge in one or more areas of spirituality or truth is to have a stronger conviction that our faith (as opposed to our knowledge) in the remaining areas is not misplaced. One definition of faith is that it is a hope in unseen things that are true (see Alma 32:21). If you only have faith or hope in something, then you will not *know* with absolute certainty if the unseen thing is actually true. You only hope it. It could happen, therefore, that you end up having a hope in an unseen thing that isn't true—in other words, misplaced faith.

A better way around the potential problem of misplaced faith is by obtaining actual knowledge in a related area. Then, knowledge by extension can help supply the more certain conviction and probability that your faith and beliefs are found in something that is, in fact, true. As we digest this and put this effort into practice, it will also spill over into our personal lives so that we apply it to others and think better of them (as long as we start with the idea that people are inherently good as children of Deity).

THE FREQUENCY OF COMPELLING WITNESSES AND WHAT THEY MEAN

We need to realize, though, that many religious ideas or truths never even go through the highest scrutiny test for us individually; compelling witnesses of truth are infrequent. Only by a compelling witness from God can a person say they absolutely know something to be true *or* false. The lack of a compelling witness does *not* indicate falsehood; it only indicates lack of certainty. You simply don't *know absolutely* one way or the other. In these cases, you either must learn to be satisfied with lower degrees of certainty on the matter, such as high degrees of faith or high degrees of belief (which can be appropriate), or you need to diligently pray to God for that perfect knowledge, while living consistently in His ways until you receive the witness or another answer from Him.

Intellectuals may argue that this "absolute" or "perfect knowledge" is ultimately subjective because it is not empirically replicable in the same way scientific experimentation and consistent results are. This, however, is false. It is not subjective. And it is replicable. Let me explain why it is not subjective from a legal perspective. First, we must consider the two ways we obtain truth in courts: (1) by direct evidence and (2) by circumstantial evidence.

Direct and Circumstantial Evidence

Direct evidence is that which comes from eyewitnesses. It comes from people who actually observed the allegedly criminal events as they were happening and those events leading up to it and/or those events after it. They saw something. They heard something. They experienced something.

Circumstantial evidence, however, is indirect because it does not rely on what specific people saw or heard, per se. Instead, it is a comparison of what circumstances were before the criminal event and/or what the circumstances were after the event, but not what the direct circumstances were *during* the event. By making these comparisons, we can arrive at a reasonable interpretation of the facts of what happened during the event. Circumstantial evidence, therefore, requires a degree of reason.

The law permits the use of circumstantial evidence, even in criminal cases, to establish the needed degree of certainty (proof beyond a reasonable doubt), much like knowledge by extension can establish higher degrees of certainty. Sometimes the circumstantial evidence is so strong that it can establish proof beyond a reasonable doubt about what crime happened and who did it. DNA evidence is an example. If, in a rape case, we find the defendant's DNA with the victim, and no one else's DNA, then we can say with a high degree of certainty that the defendant was the rapist. We still have to be persuaded, though, that the act was not consensual and that the defendant's state of mind was a criminal state of mind. The DNA by itself cannot do that. The victim or other witnesses, and perhaps other circumstantial evidence (such as broken glass at the scene reasonably indicating a fight) would have to tell us. Thus, it is generally a more direct route in establishing proof beyond a reasonable doubt by people—by witnesses—rather than by simply using reason with strong circumstantial clues.

The Circumstantial Evidence of Science

What kind of witness does science rely on? Generally, it is the witness from experimental results that can be tested, retested, and yield the same results. These empirical studies give us knowledge of our world. The empirical results, however, are fundamentally circumstantial. To get these results in science, we first form a question to be answered and then make a hypothesis of what will happen if we manipulate something in a test. Afterwards, we manipulate it and observe the results or data. We then analyze the data by comparing what the circumstances were before the test and what the resulting circumstances were after the test. We can ultimately arrive at a reasonable theory about what actually happened or will happen under the same circumstances. Afterwards, we retest our theory over and over to show that it is accurate (or at least that it has not been falsified). We try to show that we accurately made the reasonable conclusion—and that we can accurately predict what will happen under the same set of circumstances.[2] Once we show it is accurate, we have provided ourselves with what we believe is knowledge based on the high degree of certainty we've achieved. This high-degree-of-certainty knowledge (rather than absolute or perfect knowledge, but akin to beyond-a-reasonable-doubt-knowledge and experiential knowledge), however, is still subject to inaccuracies because of the dependence on theory and reason to interpret the facts and because of faulty observation skills. And it is still an indirect route to that knowledge.

THE DIRECT EVIDENCE FROM GOD

What kind of evidence is that which comes from God? Most often, it is direct evidence. God witnesses of the truth as an eyewitness by the manifestations of His Spirit, the Holy Ghost. When the Holy Ghost testifies of truth in a manner giving knowledge, there is generally no need to use an indirect route of drawing conclusions or to use reason to interpret the facts. He can tell a person exactly what a specific truth is by a compelling witness, or what the truth is by an important witness, or what the truth roughly is by a legitimate witness of the truth.

From a more legal evaluation, God's compelling witness is fundamentally more reliable, complete, trustworthy, direct, and accurate in establishing truth than any other witness (science's circumstantial evidence included) because He is direct evidence rather than evidence that requires reason to understand it. This, however, does not mean science's empirical data is not reliable, complete, trustworthy, direct, or accurate. It only means the compelling witness is more so. By a compelling witness, God can give a "perfect knowledge" (see Alma 32:21–34) that science cannot give, even with all its consistently repeatable, empirical demonstrations of what the truth should be.

The reality is, God's compelling witnesses are replicable, and they are repeated. In science, in order to obtain the exact same results in an experiment, scientists must follow precise methods. Similarly, in order to obtain a compelling witness from God, spiritual or religious "scientists" must follow strict commandments and precise directions (or methods).

When we follow God's methods with precision, the sure promise is realized: a compelling witness will come to us individually. The witness is repeated to each one of us. And the repetition may happen more than once to us individually. It is, therefore, replicable—similar to an experiment that is replicable to every scientist who tries it and follows the procedures correctly. One of the reasons compelling witnesses are infrequent, though, is that the spiritual or religious "scientists" do not follow God's commandments and directions with precision. One of His directions may be to wait because it is not His will to give you a compelling witness in a certain area at that time—possibly for your growth that He knows you personally need. Only in that way will the compelling witness not be as replicable as a scientific experiment.

A skeptical person may view this last observation of non-replicablity in some circumstances as backpedaling and weak. But let's examine the results from the scientific method and the results from unanswered prayers for certainty about truth a little more. The components of a scientific experiment neither know nor tell us that we may need to wait before learning the specific truths that will be revealed by running the experiment.

The inability of the components to know this and communicate it to us is evidence that there is no divine design behind the man-made experiment.

Conversely, the ability to *not* get an answer for questions about truth after having done everything right to receive the answer evidences a divine design—a higher intelligence appropriately does, in a paternalistic manner, what's best for us by withholding information that, if known too soon, would be harmful. Our loving God is not simply an automated machine that cranks out assembly-line products. He thinks, judges, assesses, makes decisions, and acts, which produces different results from time to time to account for conditions that only He knows.

Specific Example about Learning Things Too Quickly

If you would, consider an illustration from my own life on how gaining knowledge too soon could be harmful. This goes back to when I was very young. I wanted to know if two separate mechanical parts could fit together. I did the scientific experiment—I put the pieces together and found out that they did, in fact, fit together. But I came to know that information too soon. I got zapped. Electric shock went through my body and rattled me senseless (well, it wasn't quite that bad) because I learned things out of order. I needed to know first to hold the white cord and then try connecting the parts. Instead, I held metal prongs when connecting the parts into the living room wall.

Certainly, science can do the same things to us—we can do experiments and learn things out of order that end up being harmful because we haven't learned other important things first. Heavenly Father, on the other hand, can withhold information from us that we have properly asked for in order to protect us or help us spiritually grow in a proper manner.

Applying Scrutiny Tests as Jury Members

When it comes to personal applications in other areas of our lives, I'm not advocating that when we sit as jury members, for example, we must only come to a decision if we received a compelling witness as to the person's guilt. What I am encouraging is that we become accustomed to demanding higher degrees of certainty in our religious and personal lives before we make important decisions, especially decisions that can greatly impact the lives of others. As a jury member, this means carefully considering not only the amount and quality of evidence presented, but also considering how much certainty that evidence actually brings you. If there is a reasonable chance that the defendant is not guilty because other conditions or people may account for what happened, then you don't have knowledge and you cannot find him guilty. He is presumed and treated as innocent until and if the evidence has eliminated *all* reasonable doubt. This protects the innocent who were at the wrong place at the wrong time and look guilty through no fault of their own.

Notes

1. *Gita,* 50.
2. "A scientific method consists of the collection of data through observation and experimentation, and the formulation and testing of hypotheses ["scientific method," Merriam-Webster Dictionary].

   Although procedures vary from one field of inquiry to another, identifiable features distinguish scientific inquiry from other methodologies of knowledge. Scientific researchers propose hypotheses as explanations of phenomena, and design experimental studies to test these hypotheses. These steps must be repeatable in order to dependably predict any future results. Theories that encompass wider domains of inquiry may bind many independently derived hypotheses together in a coherent, supportive structure. . . . A linearized, pragmatic scheme of the [scientific method] is sometimes offered as a guideline for proceeding: 1. Define the question, 2. Gather information and resources (observe), 3. Form hypothesis, 4. Perform experiment and collect data, 5. Analyze data, 6. Interpret data and draw conclusions that serve as a starting point for new hypothesis, 7. Publish results, and 8. Retest (frequently done by other scientists)." Wikipedia, "Scientific Method," http://en.wikipedia.org/wiki/Scientific_method#cite_note-0, as of July 21, 2010.

SECTION III

APPLYING SCRUTINY TO PEOPLE, AND ESPECIALLY TO THE GUILTY, AND BECOMING MORE COMPASSIONATE

14

APPLYING THE SCRUTINY TESTS IN ORDER TO SCRUTINIZE PEOPLE

UNFORTUNATELY, OUT OF ALL THE TESTS FOR CERTAINTY, THE RATIONAL Basis Test, along with imagination, speculation, and make-believe, plays a huge role in people's spirituality and religion. But it doesn't stop there. It spreads. It twists their everyday views and shapes their feelings on how they think the *accused* and the *guilty* should be treated. This error carries over into their lives as jury members and they make decisions based on reasonable likelihoods rather than on the facts or lack thereof. They fail to follow what the law is as it pertains to those facts and generate what they think is appropriate for the accused or guilty person instead of simply applying the law to that set of facts.

The reality that people frequently use the lower standards of truth is not at all satisfactory, especially when it comes to making judgments about people. I've been accustomed practically all of my life to give individuals the so-called "benefit of the doubt." In other words, I frequently apply the higher evidentiary standard of "beyond a reasonable doubt." In a lot of ways, these two concepts parallel each other. To overcome the presumption of innocence that I sincerely have for each person in giving them the benefit of the doubt, I must have such an abundance of strong, clear facts to have no reasonable doubt as to the person's non-innocence. Then, even if they are guilty, I put my trust in the power that can reform individuals. As Professor Jaeger wisely stated, "The law should attempt to improve our frailties, not acknowledge them." This section focuses more on the actually guilty than the merely accused, unlike the last section.

TWO PRINCIPLES FOR JUDGING OTHERS: NO IMAGINATION AND NO GAP-FILLING

When applying the differing degrees of scrutiny to people rather than religious ideas and spiritual truths, it is important to realize two critical, interrelating principles. First, imagination and make-believe *definitely* should not be used when there *is* knowledge on spiritual or religious matters that concern our personal judgments of individuals (such as biblical principles about judging "not according to the appearance," but judging righteously (John 7:24) and "love your enemies" (Matthew 5:44)). And second, there is no need to use imagination and make-believe to fill in the gaps where we lack knowledge on the matters of judgment—we simply give the person the benefit of the doubt and continue to optimistically presume that either the person did not do the wrong or the person is not fully accountable for what he did. Either way, the person is innocent enough in that thing to be treated as fully innocent.

Keep these two principles in mind, along with the varying degrees of certainty and the Scrutiny tests, as you consider the fundamental question of this book: "How do you justify *defending* criminals if you're a dedicated member of The Church of Jesus Christ Latter-day Saints?" You can do this by asking yourself, "What do we *know* and what do we *not know* about how we should treat the guilty criminals?"

REVEALED KNOWLEDGE

One area of revealed knowledge clearly concerns how we are to treat the sinner (or guilty criminal). Yet many people make up supposedly rational—but still imagined, engineered, and manufactured—ideas about morality toward others. A man-made principle is implied in the fundamental accusation of this book: a true disciple of Christ *only* loves and protects victims of the wicked. They do not protect the wicked (or sinner) from the justice system's victimization or from unnecessary harm. These are engineered "truths." They arise from make-believe and from faulty reasoning that passes only the Rational Basis Test.

15

AN EXAMPLE OF MAKE-BELIEVE CONCERNING HOW TO TREAT THE WICKED

AN EXAMPLE FROM MY PAST ILLUSTRATES HOW I CREATED MY OWN version of morality in behaving toward the wicked. I use it because it can broadly parallel the way a lot of people create their own, similar rational morals. This example shows that my own, engineered morality would only pass the Rational Basis Test, if it would pass any tests at all. I later learned I was mistaken.

When I was in the fourth grade, I developed the bad habit of swearing. Some of my friends swore, so I decided to do it too. After a while of my conscience nagging me, I accepted the truth that swearing is wrong. But I took it a step further. I decided that I wouldn't swear at anyone or anything . . . *unless I got really mad.* That was my principle of morality. Although I imagined it, it seemed reasonable—it made sense. I used make-believe and reason to think that I was justified in swearing at someone or something if they were responsible for igniting intense anger inside me.[1]

I followed my own rules of morality and stopped swearing. One day, while I was playing on the playground, a sixth-grader made me *really* mad. Now my own version of morality applied—I could swear! After all, the Rational Basis Test approves of swearing in extreme circumstances—it's rational and based on the abstract spiritual experience of my conscience nagging me about swearing in general. So, I decided to call him a "f__er."

I continued to play until I found myself hurling out of control to the ground and eating grass. I had been slammed down by a flying side kick to my back. Turning over and looking up at my assailant, I listened to the sixth-grader yell at me, "Don't you ever call me that again!"

Looking at the sky from my vantage point below, I decided that my own rational morality was wrong.[2] I determined at that point that I would never swear again, no matter what the circumstances. I've kept that commitment ever since. (Well, I make up my own swear words instead, which I probably shouldn't do either—"making up your own swear words instead" has never passed Intermediate Scrutiny for me. My wife, Jamie, is helping me on this one).

My new commitment was not new to revealed knowledge, though. According to the scriptures, we are told: "Let no corrupt communication proceed out of your mouth" (Ephesians 4:29). This broad mandate clearly covers swearing. Generally speaking, this swearing lesson taught me that even though the wicked may unfairly offend or harm me, I am not justified in gaining revenge by offending or harming them back in some other way. There are much better solutions.

In short, when it comes to applying our own engineered, but rational, morals to others that we think are guilty of sin, justice demands better of us, compassion expects far more, and God wants us to balance both justice and compassion.

What I mean is that justice would require that we apply the rules and law that are already set forth as consequences for certain misbehavior. Compassion would allow us to apply charitable exceptions to the consequential rules and laws of justice and replace them with compassion that heals a spiritually sick soul.

Notes

1. This is a *reasonable* or rational approach to another's extreme, improper behavior, and it is loosely connected to the legitimate spiritual event I had of my conscience telling me it was wrong to swear. Thus, it can pass the Rational Basis Test as a true moral by some reasonable people's estimations.
2. Swearing when someone makes you really mad is not a correct moral principle based on this experience because it is not substantially convincing as true and it is not based on an important spiritual experience (Intermediate Scrutiny Test).

16

MAKE-BELIEVE ELSEWHERE

My own, self-generated morality isn't the only example of make-believe in the spiritual and religious worlds. Violations of the first principle of non-imagination for morals occur frequently. At one point, a person close to me wanted to found his own church—"The Church of Love." Essentially, he was going to redefine religion with what he considered to be the proper emphasis on "love," or compassion. Another man-made church. That doesn't mean it would totally lack virtue and truth and not lead followers to live a decent life—it just means that it would be limited in its ability to provide all the saving virtues and truths necessary for life as God Himself lives it. If you want those, then you need to find the church God started and presently approves of as His own.

Another subtle example of make-believe that violates the first principle of non-imagination for morals comes from a friend who introduced me to a term I'd never heard before—"Cafeteria Catholics." She, who was Catholic at the time, explained that these kinds of Catholics did not feel as if Catholicism as a whole was truly right for them. So they created their own spirituality and religion by picking and choosing church doctrines that were correct for them while also adopting virtues found outside of their church—much like going to a cafeteria and selecting food that they personally wanted to eat while rejecting those they'd prefer not to eat. The cafeteria churchgoers are essentially imagining that they can establish their own religion with their personally chosen mix of spiritual principles and behavioral actions.

RELIGION VS. KARATE

This idea of selecting certain religious truths from one religion while rejecting others from the same faith and adopting new virtues from places outside of the church reminds me of a similar (but materially different) concept that I struggled with at first when I was practicing Okinawan Shorin Ryu (Shorinkan) Karate.

I had two friends, who were brothers, attending the same karate classes as me for a time. But then they quit and went to a new style of martial arts only blocks away. They claimed it was better than mine. I began to wonder if my style of martial arts was the true one or if theirs was. One had to be better than the other, right? Then, the best one would be the true or truer one.

As I got older, however, I developed my own philosophy that it is best to master one form of martial arts and then learn others, blending the best of each form to make your own style—but doesn't this violate the first principle of non-imagination? Keep this question in mind as we continue with this example.

I received a Black Belt in my style and then went on to practice Taekwondo and then Shotokan Karate, both of which recognized my Black Belt in their styles. Learning multiple styles like this is called mixed martial arts. From my own experience and the experience of other fighters, mixed martial arts proves to be more effective than knowing only one style.

What I finally learned was that there is no one true style of martial arts. One of the reasons is that you personally, as opposed to other individuals, may master one better than the other style and, therefore, be more skilled in it and outperform others in their styles.

You may even effectively create your own form of martial arts—teach yourself better techniques from what you already know, develop more reflexes, gain more stamina, strength, and speed through different methods than taught by your original styles, live the basic philosophies of karate, and then be better than you would have been by following only the organized martial arts.

It's interesting to note that the basic philosophies of karate include the International Karate Association rules, which, if followed, provide a very decent moral life:

- Seek perfection of character
- Be faithful
- Endeavor
- Respect others
- Refrain from violent behavior

Another reason why mixed martial arts has an advantage over a single style is that each style of martial arts is lacking important techniques of self-defense that others might have, which is useful to know depending on your attacker and his style.

So, isn't spirituality and religion the same as martial arts? Isn't a person's "church" simply like a specific type of karate club for like-minded people that can be improved upon by the participants? Isn't spirituality best when you pick and choose what fits you the most, like in the karate example? In other words, what's wrong with make-believe in one's "spiritual career"[1] and combining the best that each has to offer? Isn't it true that there's no single religion that has all the truths, like no style of martial arts that has all the right self-defense moves and techniques?

The answer is no, that's not true. Religion or spirituality is not the same as martial arts because of significant source differences—one is clearly man-made and the other claims to come from Deity. When something is man-made, you can be creative until you arrive at the best combination that works for you. When something comes from Deity, however, it is objectively the best and cannot be improved upon unless by Him.

Taking the karate example, if there had been a Divine Sensei, or deified karate instructor who taught a karate class, then that style would be the one true form of martial arts. No other form could be better. But since God has never come to earth and taught martial arts, there is no single form that is superior to all others for every single individual person.

To elaborate a little more, some people will naturally be better at one form of martial arts than another. Their excellent ability in one will not necessarily translate to being as good in another form. I tried Aikido, for example, which is a form of martial arts that is performed by blending your motions with the motion of your attacker and redirecting the force of the attack rather than opposing it head-on, like karate.[2] I found myself very clumsy in this new form. I felt awkward. It wasn't for me. I didn't like the way they made my body move—it felt unnatural because I had spent almost a decade, at that point, practicing the head-on form of self-defense.

If, however, a divine being had taught Aikido, and I knew it, then I would struggle to make it work for me with the expectation that ultimately it would be best for me (and for everyone). Clearly, for me, perfecting that style of martial arts would take longer than perfecting karate since karate came so naturally to me, but the extra effort would be worth it since this martial arts form would have come from God. The same is true for the true religion to anyone who finds it awkward at first.

Extensions of the Karate Example: Where Appropriate and Where Inappropriate

The karate example can be extended to politics because politics is clearly man-made—there is no one true political party. If God created one, then there would be none better and thus it would be the true political party. Education through colleges and universities is another example—each college or university was man-made; therefore, finding the true college or university depends a lot on you and your interests, not on there being a single true college or university that can't be rivaled.

Bible Example: But a person's spirituality is not and should not be man-made. The reason is that spirituality is based on an actual standard, the Spirit of Deity, as the name "*spirit*uality" implies and denotes. The apostle Paul disparages make-believe in a person's spirituality in these words:

> Brethren, my heart's desire and prayer to God for Israel is, that they might be saved. For I bear them record that they have a zeal of God, but *not according to knowledge.*
>
> For they being ignorant of *God's* righteousness, and *going about to establish their own righteousness*, have not submitted themselves unto the righteousness of God.
>
> For Christ is the end of the law for righteousness to every one that believeth. (Romans 10:1–3, emphasis added.)

The problem Paul was dealing with in his day is no different than that in our day. Spiritual people often have a zeal for God, but their excitement and devotion to Him (or "It" in their beliefs) is not based on *knowledge* and their actions toward God are not based on actual knowledge. Instead, they are ignorant of God's position on moral behavior. Even though ignorant of this knowledge and in need of finding it, they don't go search for it. Instead, they comfortably establish their own moral behavior with what seems rational, logical, or with what makes sense. They make-believe the correct way to act toward God and people; they engineer their own morality. They create their own spirituality and do not learn God's spirituality, even though there is no need for such creativity and gap-filling in the spiritual and religious realms. The knowledge has been given to us collectively and can be repeatedly given on a personal level.

A fitting, rich-in-imagery Muslim scripture addresses the issue of make-believe, at least indirectly, in the way I read and understand the Qur'an:

> If the waters of the sea were ink with which to write the words of my Lord, the sea would surely dry up before the words of my Lord were finished. (Qur'an 18:109.)

The plain language of this verse says the Lord has so much to speak to us about that even if you were to record everything He said with a quill, dipping the quill in ink that is as great in quantity as the water found in the ocean, the ink would dry up before He was finished speaking to you.

Thus, the Lord can reveal vast amounts of information to us—important spiritual and religious information—which would leave no room for make-believe in those two areas. From a Latter-day Saint perspective, we would cite Article of Faith 9: "We believe . . . God . . . will yet reveal many great and important things pertaining to the Kingdom of God." People, though, are so accustomed to man-made things that they apply the principles of picking and choosing, or imagination and gap-filling, to areas of their lives that they should not. As discussed, spirituality and religion are two such areas. Other areas would be any that involve the need for knowledge, not the need for creativity, or make-believe, or theory, or concepts. Criminal justice is one such area—we need knowledge, not creativity, not supposition or make-believe, not personal theories, and not concepts alone.

Subjectively picking and choosing (and ignoring any divine direction that may come) will never amount to knowledge of what is right, and in areas that require knowledge of what is right, the subjective picking and choosing will lead to wrong answers and ultimately to harmful applications. The areas of criminal law and the proper ways to view and respond to criminals are areas closely linked to one's spirituality and religion. The close link between the two is why it is so important to discuss make-believe in spirituality and religion. It helps to first see how make-believe fails you if you employ it in spirituality and religion. Then it's easier to understand how that same failure occurs when applying make-believe in dealing with criminals. The failure shows itself in the coarse views people take of criminals, the development of acrimonious attitudes toward criminals, and the harsh ways people choose to treat criminals.

Book of Mormon Example: Let me give you another scriptural example of how a group of citizens failed to require knowledge for themselves on a legal matter requiring knowledge of wrong. Instead, they applied lower standards of evidence, including some great exercises in make-believe. This, in turn, produced wrongful accusations of murder and wrongful treatment of the guilty. The legal matter is intimately associated with a highly spiritual matter that had been proven through spectacular witnesses giving sufficient evidence for knowledge on the subject: the coming of Christ. This example comes from Helaman 8:22–28 and 9:1–13 at about 20 to 23 BC in the Book of Mormon. I'll break it up as we go. The prophet Nephi, who lived at the time of Christ, explained:

> Our father Lehi was driven out of Jerusalem because he testified of . . . the coming of Christ. . . .
>
> And behold, he [Christ] is God . . . .
>
> And now, seeing ye *know* these things and cannot deny them except ye shall lie, therefore in this ye have sinned, for ye have rejected all these things, notwithstanding *so many evidences* which ye have received; yea, even ye have received all things, both *things*

> *in heaven, and all things which are in the earth,* as a *witness* that they are true. (Emphasis added)

Apparently, these people had received such an abundance of evidence—from Lehi's eyewitness testimony (direct evidence) all the way to circumstantial evidence in the form of signs in heaven and earth—that Christ would come, they had knowledge on the matter, perhaps beyond a reasonable doubt knowledge. But they had "rejected the truth" and "rebelled against" their "holy God" by their "murders," "fornication," and "wickedness." As a result, they were going to be destroyed. The prophet went on to prove that the destruction was "even at your doors" by stating what no one knew—that their judge had been murdered. Five men went to determine if the prophet was correct. They said among themselves,

> Behold, now we will *know of a surety* whether this man be a prophet and God hath commanded him to prophesy such marvelous things unto us. Behold, we do not *believe* that he hath; yea, we do not *believe* that he is a prophet; nevertheless, if this thing which he has said concerning the chief judge be true, that he be dead, then will we *believe* that the other words which he has spoken are true. (Emphasis added)

Note that the men distinguished between certainty and uncertainty regarding truth. If the specific sign came true, then they would "know" the truth of Nephi as a prophet. They would not have "perfect knowledge" because they could still doubt that perhaps Nephi orchestrated the event—"Nephi must have agreed with some one to slay the judge, and then he might declare it unto us, that he might convert us unto his faith, that he might raise himself to be a great man, chosen of God, and a prophet" (Helaman 9:16). The five men also understood that they did not "believe" Nephi was a prophet. They implicitly acknowledged they had no knowledge on Nephi *not* being a prophet, only the low level of certainty as belief that he wasn't a prophet.

What they also demonstrated is knowledge by extension or, at a minimum, belief by extension. If they gained the knowledge that Nephi was a prophet, then they could believe, probably with a high degree of belief, that "the other words which he has spoken are true."

It can still be on the belief level of certainty for the other words being true because prophets can speak "presumptuously," have opinions, and make mistakes (Deuteronomy 18:22—"When a prophet speaketh in the name of the Lord, if the thing follow not, nor come to pass, that is the thing which the Lord hath not spoken, but the prophet hath spoken it presumptuously: thou shalt not be afraid of him"). The five men would need a further witness that the prophet's other teachings are true in order to have a higher degree of certainty that they are, in fact, true.

The men in this case found out that Nephi's statement regarding the chief judge was true and were "astonished exceedingly, insomuch that they fell to the earth." The confirmation of Nephi's prophecy was enough to fully convince these men to the point that they fell unconscious, which may have meant they were not only mentally acknowledging the fulfillment of Nephi's words, but also experiencing a profound witness from the Spirit that had the side effect of draining them of their strength. Compare Moses 1:10 where Moses had a profound spiritual experience: "And it came to pass that it was for the space of *many hours before Moses did again receive his natural strength* like unto man; and he said unto himself: Now, for this cause I know that man is nothing" (emphasis added) and Joseph Smith History 1:48 where Joseph Smith also had a profound spiritual experience and then afterwards, "in attempting to work as at other times, I found my *strength so exhausted as to render me entirely unable*. . . . [In] attempting to cross the fence out of the field where we were, *my strength entirely failed me, and I fell helpless* on the ground, and for a time was *quite unconscious of anything*" (emphasis added).

The next part in Helaman after the five men fell unconscious is interesting because it demonstrates the ease with which people can apply only lower degrees of certainty in critically important matters that substantially impact other people's lives. When the people saw the five fallen men, they "said among themselves: These men *are* they who have murdered the judge, and God has smitten them that they could not flee from us" (emphasis added). After making such hasty conclusions, they "laid hold on them, and bound them and cast them into prison."

When the people were questioned by the others, who had known about the five men, the people responded, "Concerning this five whom ye say ye have sent, we know not; but there are five *who are the murderers*, whom we have cast into prison" (emphasis added). When the others checked on the "murderers," they discovered they were the five innocent men who were sent.

This account shows how make-believing people take coincidence to mean divine intervention when there is no evidence of divine intervention. First, people see their ruler has been killed. Second, they see a group of people unconscious by the ruler. Third, they draw the unwarranted, completely conclusive, and firm speculation that the unconscious group of people is responsible for the murder, which they think is reasonable. And fourth, they attribute the unconsciousness to a deliberate act of God on them for causing the ruler's death, even though such an act of God of a similar nature has never been recorded in all of scriptural history—He didn't do that to Cain for killing Able, not to King David for killing Uriah, not to wicked pharaoh killing Israelites, and, in addition, He didn't do that to Judas Iscariot after his effort to betray Christ to execution.

Notes

1. *Gita,* p. 50.
2. Wikipedia, "Aikido," http://en.wikipedia.org.wiki/Aikido, as of July 21, 2010.

17

SCRIPTURAL JUSTIFICATIONS FOR DEFENDING CRIMINALS

THIS CHAPTER WILL POINT OUT MUCH OF THE REVEALED KNOWLEDGE on how we should personally judge and treat criminal individuals. The revealed knowledge goes to the heart of Mr. Fey's question, "Taylor, how do you justify *defending* criminals if you're a dedicated member of The Church of Jesus Christ of Latter-day Saints?" As you read the verses, remember to include "criminals" in with "sinners" because there is no significant difference between the two in how we should think about and react to them. The reason is that sinners violate God's law, which in many instances also violates man's law. Criminals violate man's law, which in many instances also violates God's laws. In fact, every criminal may potentially be a sinner because of Article of Faith 12: "We believe in . . . obeying, honoring, and sustaining the law." Thus, for all intents and purposes here, sinners and criminals can be used interchangeably.

CHRIST IS OUR PATTERN

To begin our analysis, we first have to realize whose behavior to pattern in acting toward others. Our greatest exemplar, Jesus Christ, showed us the way to live, for "Jesus saith unto him, I am the way" (John 14:6) and "I have given you an example, that ye should do as I have done to you" (John 13:15).

With these scriptures as our foundation, the important questions that need to be answered before we can answer Mr. Fey's question are "What was Christ's way of life?" and "What did Christ do to people?" so that we can follow His actions.

Not Condemn: According to the scriptural account in the New Testament, He "gave himself . . . that he might deliver us from this present evil world, according to the will of God and our Father" (Galatians 1:4) for "God sent *not* his Son into the world *to condemn* the world; but that the world through him might be saved" (John 3:17; emphasis added). As I use the word, *condemn* is to pass judgment, and, implicitly, to damn and punish as a result of the judgment. Christ did not come to condemn an evil world. He came to deliver and save it. Specifically, "Christ Jesus came into the world to *save* sinners" (1 Timothy 1:15; emphasis added).

Thus, knowledge recorded in the scriptures teaches us to do two things: follow the example of Jesus Christ in living the way He did, and not personally condemn sinful or criminal people as He did not, but try to deliver and save them as He did. Accordingly, we do not condemn them in our thoughts and viewpoints about them. We individually do not condemn them in the ways we treat them.

Christ's Criticisms: This is not to say Christ did not criticize or rebuke certain people, such as calling some "hypocrites" during His ministry. Matthew 23 is an example of strong criticism that He leveled against others. Criticizing and condemning are different, though. Criticizing does not inflict a punishment for that which is criticized. Furthermore, a person who has all knowledge is certainly qualified to make strong criticisms. We are not omniscient and we need to be careful about trying to criticize like Christ did because those criticisms require knowledge of what the others knew. Getting into the mind of a person is difficult. It is the most difficult aspect of proving an accused person guilty. They have to not only do the guilty act, but also do so with a guilty mind. They had to *intend* to do it, *know* they were doing it, or be *reckless* about doing it. Those are mental states that must be proven in order for there to be a crime.

Condemnation for Higher Powers: We leave necessary, condemning punishment to a higher power, such as the government, for example. Arguably, whenever Christ did punish people—for example, at the temple with the money changers (John 2:14–15—"And when he had made a scourge of small cords, he drove them all out of the temple, and the sheep, and the oxen; and poured out the changers' money, and overthrew the tables")—He was issuing necessary correction as a higher power. He never expressly taught us to do the same in punishing others. The only time in scripture that we are clearly counseled to individually act or speak in these ways is when we are directly prompted to do so by Deity: "Reproving betimes with sharpness, *when moved upon by the Holy Ghost*; and then showing forth afterwards an increase of love toward him whom thou hast reproved" (D&C 121:43).

Focus on Healing "Souls": As our own default rule, we focus on remedies more than penalties—remedies that have the power to reform, or the power to "save a *soul* from death" (James 5:20, emphasis added). We focus on remedies especially when we consider that Jesus said, "Whosoever committeth sin is the *servant* of sin" (John 8:34, emphasis added) and that "the Lord, the God of hosts, the God of Israel" said, "Wherefore commit ye this great evil *against your souls*?" (Jeremiah 44:7, emphasis added). Through sin, people become slaves and end up harming their own souls. Like our Master, though, we are to save the sinners from spiritual death, and save the criminals from a similar demise. They are *souls*, not devils.

Why do Christ and the Father wish us to *not* condemn the "scum of the earth," as I've heard them described to me before? Don't these people deserve a just condemnation from each one of us?

A good answer to those questions is in Christ's response to the Pharisees. They wanted the righteous and law-abiding people to abandon sinners and criminals and treat them as of lesser value than the religious. The scriptures describe the event and the answer as follows:

> And when the Pharisees saw it, they said unto his disciples, Why eateth your Master with . . . *sinners*? But when Jesus heard that, he said unto them, They that be whole need not a physician, but *they that are sick*. But *go ye and learn what that meaneth*, I will have *mercy*, and not sacrifice: for *I am* not *come to call* the righteous, but *sinners to repentance*. Matthew 9:11–13.[1] Emphasis added.

What did Christ want us to learn from this statement? He specifically said, "[G]o ye and learn what *that* meaneth" (emphasis added), referring to what he had already said about the sick needing a physician. What, then, is the meaning of the "sick" needing a "physician"?

As I understand it from these verses, Christ sees Himself as a doctor to heal people with illnesses. There is deep meaning to this attitude about who He is and what He does; do doctors turn patients away who are sick, whether they are sick by chance or by their own choices? No. Doctors try to heal their patients regardless of the reason they are sick. In the emergency room, physicians don't tell a suicidal patient, "Are you mangled because you intentionally drove the car off the cliff—because if you are, I'm not going to try to heal you." Physicians ignore the intentional aspect of what caused the injuries or sicknesses. Their attitude is to treat the injuries or sickness the same as those contracted involuntarily. The remedy—healing—is the same. If it is the same without regard to the voluntariness of any wrongdoing, then it seems that all sicknesses are treated by physicians as if they are *involuntary* or as good as involuntary. If Christ compares Himself to a physician, then it appears that the Master Healer is choosing to maintain this *attitude* (not *acknowledgment*) that sin is as good as an involuntarily contracted disease to be healed rather than a voluntarily chosen act to be condemned.

Let me clarify. Certainly we are not spiritually sick as we come into this world. This malady is developed. Our God knows this and even acknowledges this through His prophets. Moroni taught, "Behold I say unto you that this thing shall ye teach—repentance and baptism unto those who are *accountable* and *capable of committing sin* . . . little children need no repentance, neither baptism. . . . *[L]ittle* children are *alive in Christ*, even from the foundation of the world" (Moroni 8:10–12, emphasis added). Accountability and capability for sin are essential elements to committing actual "sin." If either one is missing, so is the sin. As we get older, we typically become accountable and capable of committing sin and develop spiritual sickness in one way or another.

But even though we develop spiritual sickness for whatever reason (whether by our own choices, by victimization from others' wrongdoings, or by ignorance), that does not disqualify us from healing.

What I gather from Christ's statement is that the *attitude* toward a person's willful misconduct needs to be the same as if it were no fault of their own; they committed the wrong while sleepwalking, for example, and injured themselves. The *attitude* is one of healing regardless of a person's voluntary acts to commit sin. Sin, or voluntary wrongdoing, especially is harmful, which is even more reason to want to heal them.

Maintain the Better Attitude: This rather optimistic *attitude* about sinners needing healing is in contradiction to the emphatic viewpoint we take in modern society on our ability to choose (but we still need to acknowledge that our own and other persons' sins are voluntary, yet our attitude toward another person's sin must be different in order to best heal them). There is wisdom in this optimistic kind of *attitude* because, as we take pride in our independence, autonomy, and self-sufficient agency, we are oftentimes led to the attitude of condemnation for the sinner. We conclude that someone willfully chose 100 percent to commit a crime or sinful act. We give no regard to contributing causes that may decrease that percentage by some or, in rare cases, all percentage points. Giving no regard to other contributing causes can make us lack sympathy for the sinner, which is contrary to how Christ felt toward sinners.

An example of contributing causes that lessen the degree of guilt—but do not take it totally away—is from a client named Eric. He had leased his car to a lady who needed to use it. After a couple months, she abandoned Eric's car, and he had no idea where it was. About six months later, a company contacted him and said they were going to take the car's title if he didn't pick the car up from their lot and pay for the months of rental time that it had spent on their fenced grounds. Eric thought it was unfair that he had to basically buy his car back for doing nothing wrong—why should he pay for rental space that he didn't even know about and certainly didn't agree to? Why does he have to pay for someone else's wrongdoing? It was especially unfair to him since he was a victim of crime—the lady had exercised *unauthorized* control over his vehicle by abandoning it.

So, in a brilliant stroke of reason and as a victim acting out inappropriately, Eric decided to break into the lot and reclaim *his* car. So he and his wife went to the grounds, picked a lock on the fence, and drove his car away. Later, the company owner called Eric and left him a message. He said he knew he had taken his car because a camera on the lot recorded him breaking in and getting it. He said he was calling the police and that he better return the vehicle.

Somewhat panicked, Eric called me and asked what to do. I advised him to take his car back to the lot immediately. I told him I'd arrive there with him and see if we could prevent this event from becoming an auto theft and burglary crime. Shortly after we all arrived, the police officer came too. After some negotiating and Eric relinquishing his car completely to the company, the company told the officer it did not want any charges filed against Eric. The police officer lectured Eric but didn't file any report. If he had, Eric would have been facing felony charges, up to about thirty years in prison, and a fine of up to about $35,000. Realistically, even after righting the wrong by simply giving his car to the company and paying any required rent, he would have pled guilty to at least one felony. Then he probably would have been put on probation for thirty-six months and would have had to pay a few thousand dollars as a fine to the court with monthly installments. And he would be risking jail time for any violation during the probation. Violations of probation can occur simply by forgetting to update your address with the court, by paying your fine a day late, or sometimes by committing common traffic offenses, like speeding. All this would have happened if the negotiations hadn't gone well and the police officer had decided to file a police report to the prosecutor. My client learned his lesson without having a felony on his record and the court slapping him with thousands of dollars in fines.

Interestingly, during the negotiation process, we discovered that the company owner's claim of knowing that Eric took the car was a bluff. He didn't know. There were no cameras. When the owner saw the car was missing, he looked on the ground where the car had been. The key was still there. The company kept the keys underneath the cars in order to keep them together. Because the key was still there, the only way the car could have been driven off the lot was by someone who had another key to the car: the owner. So, using deduction skills, a little luck, and a small threat, the company owner got the car back.

This case shows that there are other causes for criminal conduct beyond simply the volition of the criminal. A victim acting out inappropriately is one such example. When a person has been victimized, the victimization is a condition that is beyond his control, which can *influence* (not necessarily compel) him to act criminally.

Here, it seemed logical to Eric to retake his own property without someone holding it for ransom because he was a victim—he had done nothing wrong, yet he was being penalized for it with his own property. His subsequent misconduct was, therefore, somewhat understandable and not as guilty as someone's misconduct of stealing a vehicle that did *not* belong to him and that was *not* wrongfully taken from him in the first place.

Other examples are when abused spouses lash out at their abusers above and beyond what is required for self-defense, similar to my lesbian client. She stabbed her former boyfriend in the back with a kitchen knife, puncturing his lung, after he frightened her one night by knocking on her door and running down the flight of stairs by her front door. She chased him in hot pursuit when there was no reason to chase him. She had snapped. She had been repeatedly abused by this man in the past. He had thrown her on the hood of his car and bruised her days before. These types of injuries were not uncommon. His mistreatment of her led her to hate men and firmly establish herself as a lesbian. Her physical assault on him was not simply out of an unprovoked, deliberate attempt to harm him. It was a delayed response to the compounding abuses that he had inflicted on her. Her guiltiness, therefore, was lessened by the contributing cause of being an ongoing victim of crime.

But, with the pride in the autonomy that we have, we go on to say that people are 100 percent accountable for their poor choices, without regard for any mitigating factors that may lessen the degree to which they are accountable. But Christ acknowledged that there are times when a person's sin does not remain as a sin: "Jesus said unto them, If ye were blind, ye should have no sin: but now ye say, We see; therefore your sin remaineth" (John 9:41). Not seeing or knowing the wrong, and doing it, produces *no* accountability for sin.

The guilty mind must be present for sin to occur just as it must be in committing crime.

With the attitude we commonly develop, however, we often say that a wrong-doing person deserves punishment. Then we apply a different remedy to the situation, such as retributive penalties over rehabilitative measures. If we thought they were *not* fully accountable, or if we maintained the attitude they were not fully accountable due to some sickness, then our remedy for the aberrant behavior would be different. Retributive penalties as a remedy for the situation are not healing. They engender bitterness more often than contrition. Retribution is the remedy of deterrence through an "eye-for-an-eye" justice. It's revenge. Pure punishment for the wrongdoer. But that's not the attitude a healing physician takes toward his sick patients who are and aren't responsible for their sicknesses—the physician doesn't spank those who are willfully sick and only heal those who are not willfully sick.

Whether it is true that anyone's spiritual sickness is actually involuntary is not the focus—it's not what Christ concentrates on when He wishes to heal. His *attitude* toward and *general healing* of criminals and their misconduct is no different than toward the innocent who have been victimized: the sinners and victims are all sick and His treatment is to heal it, regardless of why they are sick. To me, that shows the *attitude* (not *acknowledgment*) that sin is more an involuntary contracted disease than a willfully chosen act. He acknowledges, however, that sin is (1) a willfully chosen act or (2) a deliberate omission: "That which breaketh a law, and abideth not by law, but seeketh to become a law unto itself, and willeth to abide in sin, and altogether abideth in sin, cannot be sanctified by law, neither by mercy, justice, nor judgment" (D&C 88:35), and "Therefore to him that knoweth to do good, and doeth it not, to him it is sin" (James 4:17).

Christ's attitude, for the clear majority of the time, is one of compassion toward others who need His healing hands—He died for them all and experienced the full punishment of their sins so they could all be healed, whether they were sinfully sick, or sick through victimization, or sick due to lacking God's law.

His attitude is not an "eye-for-an-eye" revenge and condemnation on the willful sinner. He declared, "Ye have heard that it hath been said, An eye for an eye, and a tooth for a tooth: But I say unto you . . . [l]ove your enemies, bless them that curse you, do good to them that hate you, and pray for them which despitefully use you, and persecute you" (Matthew 5:38–39, 44). If it's not His attitude to maintain an "eye for an eye" justice, and if we're to follow Him, then that's not the attitude we should adopt either. We should adopt His attitude that sin should be healed and that crime should be seen *more like* a physical sickness—essentially an involuntary misfortune—*because it makes no difference to us in our reactions; we heal them regardless of the guilt involved.* If it is regardless of guilt, then we are ignoring the intentional aspects. If we ignore the intentional aspects that may be there, then we are demonstrating an attitude that the sickness *is* unintentional or involuntary or at least *as good as* unintentional or involuntary. This optimistic *attitude* will enable us to truly heal someone guilty of crime or sin by applying the correct remedy needed.

Negative Effects of a Realistic Attitude: It is no stretch of the imagination that if we have an underlying attitude of wishing to punish a person for intentional wrongdoings, then we will be prevented from effectively healing them. So criminal defense attorneys, who are in the best position to advocate for healing the defendant, need to view their actually *guilty* clients as more involuntarily sick so they can truly endeavor to get them healed. Otherwise, the knee-jerk reaction in us will likely prevent us from zealously advocating their cause for rehabilitation, which may, in order for them to be healed, exclude typical punishments like incarceration with other inmates.

Second Witness to the Focus on Healing "Souls": What I also find significant is that this idea of perceiving criminals and sinners as sick and in need of healing rather than in need of pure condemnation is repeated in another book of revealed scripture. In more forceful introductory language, the Book of Mormon records the words of our Savior as follows:

> *Listen to the words of Christ,* your Redeemer, your Lord and *your God.* Behold, I came into the world not to call the righteous but sinners to repentance; the whole need no *physician*, but they that are *sick.* (Moroni 8:8, emphasis added.)

Thus, in the mouth of these two scriptural witnesses, the New Testament of the Bible and the Book of Mormon, the Lord has more convincingly established with revealed knowledge that sinners and criminals are to be treated as if they are spiritually sick, which *sickness* could have caused their misconduct. They are to be healed regardless of their culpability. So, it bears repeating that that's the same attitude we individually need to adopt on a general basis because we are to follow His example and ways. The Spirit can lead us to depart from this general attitude when necessary. But, even then, we are still to show forth an increased amount of love afterwards (see D&C 121:43).

The *knowledge*[2] given to us in the scriptures tells us that criminals generally need the compassionate, healing hands of a doctor calling them to willfully choose a particular course of medical conduct that will heal them (in other words, repentance). They do not normally need the condemning hands of disciplinarians and executioners (perhaps they only need one set of condemning hands, and that from the higher power, such as the federal, state, county, or city governments, church disciplinary councils, or Deity).

Love without Exception: Some may wonder if this compassionate attitude that Christ has, which I've painted here, is consistent with His other teachings. I believe it is. He taught, without exception, to "love one another" (John 15:12). Actually, it is more proper to state that He *commanded* us to "love one another" (John 15:17—"These things I command you, that ye love one another"), and He ordered us to do so *without any exceptions*. The specific language of the revealed knowledge is as follows: "This is my commandment, That ye love one another, *as* I have loved you" (John 15:12, emphasis added). He did not limit His command to "love one another *as long as they are not criminals to you*."

If we are to love others *as* Christ did, then did He truly love others without exception? Yes, He did, and He taught it: "Ye have heard that it hath been said, Thou shalt love thy neighbour, and hate thine enemy" (Matthew 5:43). This is the world's engineered morality to love all others except those who are your enemies, which would include the criminal enemy. "But I say unto you, Love your [criminal] enemies, bless them that curse you [through crime], do good to them that hate you [as shown by their crime], and pray for them which despitefully use you [in their crime], and persecute you [with crime]" (Matthew 5:44).

The course of conduct that Christ outlined for us is one which God the Father also follows:

> Love your enemies . . . [t]hat ye may be the children of your Father which is in heaven: for he maketh his sun to rise on the evil and on the good, and sendeth rain on the just and on the unjust.
>
> For if ye love them which love you, what reward have ye? do not even the publicans the same?
>
> And if ye salute your brethren only, what do ye more than others? do not even the publicans so?
>
> Be ye therefore perfect, even as your Father which is in heaven is perfect. (Matthew 5:44–48)

We are to be perfect in the same way God the Father is perfect; we are to love the just and the unjust, the law-abiding citizen and the criminal. As applied to defense attorneys, we are to give the same benefit of zealous legal defense to the innocent as well as to the guilty, just as God gives the same benefits of the sun's rising on the good and on the evil, and He gives the same life-giving rain to benefit both the just citizen and the unjust criminal.

Love without Exception by Blessing Others: We have another witness from the Gospel of Luke that goes into further detail about how to *treat* the criminal. Christ did not simply teach, "Love the sinner, hate the sin." He taught about proactive efforts of love:

> But I say unto you which hear, Love your enemies, *do good* to them which hate you,
>
> *Bless* them that curse you, and *pray for* them which despitefully use you.
>
> And unto him that smiteth thee on the one cheek *offer also the other*; and him that taketh away thy cloke *forbid not to take thy coat also.*
>
> *Give to every man* that asketh of thee; and of him that taketh away thy goods *ask them not again.*
>
> And as ye would that men should do to you, *do ye also to them likewise.*

> For if ye love them which love you, what thank have ye? for sinners also love those that love them.
>
> And if ye do good to them which do good to you, what thank have ye? for sinners also do even the same.
>
> And if ye lend to them of whom ye hope to receive, what thank have ye? for sinners also lend to sinners, to receive as much again.
>
> But love ye your enemies, and *do good*, and *lend, hoping for nothing again*; and your reward shall be great, and ye shall be the children of the Highest: for he is *kind unto the unthankful and to the evil.*
>
> Be ye therefore *merciful, as your Father* also is merciful.
>
> *Judge not*, and ye shall not be judged: *condemn not*, and ye shall not be condemned: *forgive*, and ye shall be forgiven. (Luke 6:27–37, emphasis added).

Loving the sinner or the criminal does not mean merely forming the mental opinion that you "love" them. It does not mean simply doing them no harm. It means being actively "kind . . . to the evil," as stated above in Luke 6:35. Being kind to the criminal means that you actually "do good" to them, "bless" them in your speech instead of curse them, "pray for them," offer the other cheek instead of retaliate against them for direct wrongs they have committed against you or others, give generously to criminals that steal from you or to those who only ask of you, lend and don't expect to have anything returned to you, and do to criminals what you wish would be done to you.

Loving the sinner or criminal also means that we are merciful to the criminal, even if the criminal justly deserves what we consider to be the pre-set punishment for their wrong(s). Loving the criminal enemy also means not making final judgments about them that won't change. It also means not condemning them. All of this is what loving the sinner or the criminal means on a *personal* basis (not a governmental basis, such as prosecuting those accused of breaking society's laws, which is fully appropriate).

Isn't a criminal defense attorney's entire job to protect his client from *unfair* final judgments and condemnations, just as Christ taught us to avoid making? How does a criminal defense attorney pleading on behalf of his client's *just* rights or for *legal* leniency violate these admonitions to love the criminal by not forbidding your cloak, so to speak, when the criminal has taken your coat? Is it not a way of being kind to the evil person regardless of their guiltiness—a kindness that's not deserved—a kindness that is the best hope for healing?

Kindness Gives the Best Hope for Rehabilitation That Stops Victimization: You may argue that treating guilty criminals in these ways with kindness empowers the criminal to simply victimize someone else. It is a legitimate concern and a valid one. Those who advocate this concern typically take the stance that criminals must be stopped by incapacitation—we should force them to stop their criminal behavior and, thereby save victims, by sending the criminals to jail or prison.

But, for most criminals, there is still a better route to take that will achieve the same end. Protecting victims by the punishment of physically incapacitating the criminal does nothing to heal the criminal (not usually at least. There are those who take the time in prison or jail to think about what they did and resolve not to do it again. But, usually, if they were sick enough to do the crime, then they are probably too sick to heal themselves after the crime). If anything, the incarceration is more likely to make the criminal better able to victimize once he learns from the other incapacitated criminals and is released from incarceration. The better route is the one a defense attorney takes. He pleads for remedies, not coerced restraint.

The remedies, hopefully, will *convert* the sinner, *save* a soul from spiritual death, and "hide a multitude of sins"—a far better outcome than simply punishing the criminal in the hopes that it will deter him from later misconduct. It protects from future victimization, just as physical incapacitation would, but even better because it is the best hope for a long-term change. I base this stance on James 5:20, which reads, "Let him know, that he which converteth [not "*punisheth*"] the sinner from the error of his way shall save a soul from death, and shall hide a multitude of sins." The defense attorney's pleading on behalf of the criminal is, therefore, a method of asking for a form of proper mercy or leniency and appropriate forgiveness than can heal and convert him when raw justice may demand a different outcome, one that has less hope for the future. In essence, trying to convert the criminal is like trying to do effective missionary work that seeks to convert lost or hungering souls to the salvation of Jesus Christ.

LOVE IN THE MANNER CHRIST LOVED

Up until this scripture in Luke on how to love others, I have stressed that loving others includes loving all others, even criminals. But there is another important feature of loving others that must be emphasized. Recall what Christ commanded: "This is my commandment, That ye *love* one another, *as I have* loved you" (John 15:12, emphasis added). Not only are we to love everyone, including criminals, just as Christ did, but we are to love them in the *way* that Christ loved them in His actions, not only in His verbal teachings. Specific examples will follow.

If we live this higher commandment, then we are not to make-believe or engineer what we think is the proper *manner* of loving others. We are commanded to love others in the same manner that Christ showed individuals—as healing physicians—"*as* I have loved you." The question, "What would Jesus do?" is the correct approach to loving others.

I believe this command to love the way Jesus loved is potentially a higher law than the Golden Rule, which is to treat others the way you would like to be treated or, in other words, to love your neighbor as yourself. Christ termed His rule a "*new* commandment I give unto you" (John 13:34). We are to love our neighbor *as the mortal Jesus Christ loved people*. This is an objective standard instead of the subjective standard of how you would like to be loved.

Let's explore how our Savior loved people during His ministry. As we saw in the beginning of the chapter, Christ verbally taught us to love without condemnation for sinners and to love them with an attitude that they are spiritually sick and need compassionate care and direction on how to be healed. But in John 15:12, we learn that we are to love others in the same manner Christ did. This knowledge about how Christ specifically loved others is recorded in the scriptures. Some of those examples are as follows:

1. Christ's Reaction to the Two Criminals and to the Crucifiers: Loving Patience, Kindness, and Forgiveness

> And there were also two other, malefactors [Greek: criminals], led with him to be put to death. And when they were come to the place, which is called Calvary, there they crucified him, and the malefactors, one on the right hand, and the other on the left. Then said Jesus, Father, forgive them [the crucifiers]; for they know not what they do. . . . And one of the malefactors which were hanged railed on him, saying, If thou be Christ, save thyself and us. But the other answering rebuked him, saying, Dost not thou fear God, seeing thou art in the same condemnation? And we indeed justly; for we receive the due reward of our deeds: but this man hath done nothing amiss. And he said unto Jesus, Lord, remember me when thou comest into thy kingdom. And Jesus said unto him, Verily I say unto thee, To day shalt thou be with me in paradise. (Luke 23:32–43, clarifications added).

In this example, Christ was in the presence of two actual criminals who were genuinely guilty of their crimes. They had harmed individuals by their criminal misconduct. When one criminal apparently tried to insult Christ for His claims of being the Messiah, Christ did not respond with any harshness nor did He scold or condemn the unbelieving criminal. Instead, He allowed the challenge to His authority and took no offense to it. He exhibited silent, loving patience. Then, when the other criminal pled for mercy, Christ responded with proactive love. He did not speak any censuring words to the second truly guilty criminal. He was kind. He offered him words of hope regarding paradise despite the fact that the second criminal had committed a crime worthy of death—he had harmed someone or others so severely that, under their laws, his life had to be taken. In essence, Christ reacted as a spiritual physician to this repentant criminal, even though the criminal had harmed at least one other, giving him the healing hope of a better future.

From this example, we see that Christ condemned neither criminal, even though they were both guilty of actions egregious enough to merit capital punishment. He was kind and loving to the "scum of the earth," a term people frequently use to rationalize cruel considerations and treatment of law-offending individuals.

In addition to this love toward the criminals that Jesus showed, He also expressed loving forgiveness to those involved in nailing Him on the cross. He did this by asking the Father to grant them forgiveness for their wrongful acts against Him, even when none of them had asked Christ for mercy like the second criminal had. Thus, like a doctor, He pursued ways to heal the people from their disorders, not condemn them like an executioner would.

The work of a criminal defense attorney is ultimately the same—if he is representing clients who are guilty, and have pled guilty, then his next obligation is to ensure that his client does not receive an unfair punishment, one that would amount to "cruel and unusual punishments" (Eighth Amendment to the U.S. Constitution) from being more severe than deserved or necessary.

Reasons for Punishment: There are multiple reasons for punishments, which include: (1) retribution or revenge on the criminal; (2) incapacitation of the criminal for the protection of society; (3) rehabilitation of the criminal; (4) specific deterrence for the criminal from doing the crime again or general prevention of the criminal act by the rest of society; and (5) restoration to the victim(s) of what was lost because of the crime.

Oftentimes, in my experience, the fair punishment is one that will help effectively rehabilitate the criminal rather than penalize him as retribution for the crime. The recidivism rate of criminals is an indication that they are not receiving effective rehabilitation, either because the only remedy they received was pure punishment without the rehabilitation or they received ineffective rehabilitation. A cynical view would be that the recidivism rate is so high because most criminals enjoy being evil. It may be true. Do we know that for sure? No. If we don't know, we give them the benefit of the doubt. Thus, let's assume the poor recidivism rate is due to ineffective rehabilitation, not to people enjoying outright rebellion and harming others. If we *know* a specific, repeat criminal who does enjoy harming others, then we can make that accusation *toward him*, not to repeat criminals in general. There are more reasons for being a repeat criminal than simply wanting to harm others or being outright rebellious.

Effective Rehabilitation: Part of an effective rehabilitation would be helping the convicted criminals out of living circumstances and social situations that many times prompt illegal behavior. They need to see and know by their own experience that there is a better way to live, that it is worth it, and that it is within their reach.

Pursuing an effective remedy in this way is more patient and loving than seeking a mere penalty because it accomplishes the same purpose, but with greater care for the criminal. That purpose is to prevent further criminal activity: deterrence. Thus, punishment that serves as a remedy will *reform* somebody from doing it again; punishment that serves as a penalty simply *discourages* somebody from doing it again. Because they both can achieve the same goal of deterrence, the better way of fashioning punishment should be to *rehabilitate* the spiritually diseased criminal individual for the love it exhibits. Furthermore, rehabilitating can heal him permanently, so that he chooses to do right of his own volition—it doesn't merely discourage the sick criminal from doing the wrong act because, ultimately, the discouragement will *not* have the power to overcome future circumstances and social situations that strongly tempt him from doing it again. But a reformed person could overcome those circumstances.

To summarize briefly this portion of our analysis as it applies to the question of this book:

- Christ was and is a physician, not an executioner
- In defending actual criminals, I seek to do what Christ does—to heal

Essentially, I try to be a spiritual physician that seeks to heal and rehabilitate the guilty criminal instead of condemn and hunt for retribution on the criminal as an executioner would.

Prosecution Can Also Focus on Healing "Souls": Interestingly, the opposite of a criminal defense attorney does not mean the opposite of what Christ did. A prosecutor can also seek for the same outcomes—to heal and rehabilitate the criminal—and, thereby, be a spiritual physician to the criminally sick. Judges and juries can do the same. Our entire system of justice can work toward being as Christlike as the system of spiritual healing that Christ performed. It is already set up to allow such outcomes. We need to take better advantage of the system by augmenting the effectiveness and availability of rehabilitative relief.

2. Christ's Reaction to the People Assaulting Him with Weapons During the Night: Loving Inquiries, Healing, and Compassion

Judas then, having received a band of men and officers from the chief priests and Pharisees, cometh thither with lanterns and torches and weapons.

Jesus therefore, knowing all things that should come upon him, went forth, and said unto them, Whom seek ye?

They answered him, Jesus of Nazareth. Jesus saith unto them, I am he. And Judas also, which betrayed him, stood with them.

As soon then as he had said unto them, I am he, they went backward, and fell to the ground.

Then asked he them again, Whom seek ye? And they said, Jesus of Nazareth.

Jesus answered, I have told you that I am he: if therefore ye seek me, let these go their way:

That the saying might be fulfilled, which he spake, Of them which thou gavest me have I lost none.

Then Simon Peter having a sword drew it, and smote the high priest's servant, and cut off his right ear. The servant's name was Malchus.

Then said Jesus unto Peter, Put up thy sword into the sheath: the cup which my Father hath given me, shall I not drink it? (John 18:3–11)

And Jesus answered and said, Suffer ye thus far. And he touched his ear, and healed him. (Luke 22:51)

Then said Jesus unto him, Put up again thy sword into his place: for all they that take the sword shall perish with the sword.

Thinkest thou that I cannot now pray to my Father, and he shall presently give me more than twelve legions of angels?

But how then shall the scriptures be fulfilled, that thus it must be?

In that same hour said Jesus to the multitudes, Are ye come out as against a thief with swords and staves for to take me? I sat daily with you teaching in the temple, and ye laid no hold on me. (Matthew 26:52–55).

Christ did nothing to harm His attackers who illegally came at night with weapons to forcefully apprehend Him. Justice would have permitted it in defending Himself. But, in fact, He reacted with kindness instead. He inquired why, if He had done something illegal, the attackers did not seek to capture Him during the day when He was peacefully teaching in the temple. Here, He sought to diagnose the problem. In this way, He acted as a physician. He also applied preventive care when He sought to protect the disciples who were with Him by asking the attackers to let them go and only take Him.

During this encounter, Christ literally performed the *same acts* that a physician would when He physically healed one of His assaulters by miraculously reattaching a severed ear. From most people's perspectives, Malchus, the soldier who had been injured, did not deserve the compassionate love Christ showed him because he was illegally capturing the Lord by violent means. Christ, though, was a physician to sinners and would heal them without regard to the voluntariness of their wrongdoing. In the end, Christ found it more important to be assaulted, wrongfully imprisoned, gruesomely tortured, and ultimately crucified than to fight back against the criminal misconduct He suffered.

For Christ, the duty of accomplishing His Father's mission was more of a medicine for these untried criminals than fighting their injustices. Simply suffering the betrayal and harm from His attackers' hands was more of a medicine to them than physically defending Himself from their cruelty. He knew that reacting with violence would only create more violence, which would be the antithesis of treating the criminals as diseased patients. Instead, He treated them like they were sick; He didn't use violence because violence does not cure or heal a sick person. Kind, patient, compassionate treatment does, just as He exhibited here.

Christ did not love these criminals because they were loveable. He loved them because they were spiritually sick and because He was sent to be their Physician. And, taking this a step further, all of us must do likewise if we are to be true followers of Christ. Even a criminal defense attorney is in a position to take this step—the defense attorney works on a personal level with sinners and criminals, petitioning for a remedy from the courts for their wrong and not seeking a penalty to merely condemn them for their misconduct and gain revenge or retribution.

Necessary Self-Defense Can Be Appropriate: Some may wonder if I, a black belt in self-defense, am advocating a non–self-defense or a pacifist approach to all situations. I'm not. There are two values that we are trying to achieve: the protection of the innocent; and the healing of the guilty. At times, these two values come into conflict and one has to be sacrificed over the other. If this happens, then the priority value is the protection of the innocent. Defending yourselves, your family, your religion, and your nation is, at times, the only way to protect the innocent. Alma 46:12 tells of Captain Moroni preparing to lead his people to war: "And it came to pass that he rent his coat; and he took a piece thereof, and wrote upon it—In memory of our God, our religion, and freedom, and our peace, our wives, and our children—and he fastened it upon the end of a pole." Here, the values were competing. But, when the two values are *not* mutually exclusive, which is most of the time, then you work to achieve both. It is during the endeavor to accomplish both values that violence is clearly no medicine for the guilty.

Pure Retribution Is Never Appropriate for Disciples: Additionally, defense is not retribution. It is the protection of self and others. Retribution is pure revenge for no other purpose than to return evil for evil. And I am saying that retribution is not the right choice for a proper remedy if we are to follow Christ's example.

Perhaps this is a bold position to take. One of the common purposes for criminal penalties is retribution. Retribution is essentially punishment for the sake of pure punishment—a type of revenge, or eye-for-an-eye mentality. It is a form of pure justice. Many people feel retribution is appropriate for those criminals who are beyond rehabilitation. So, am I suggesting that such a purpose is un-Christlike—that pure justice in this form is not Christian?

To answer that, let me ask you a question: did you ever read about Christ, in His mortal ministry, punishing others for the sake of retaliation, revenge, or pure punishment? I don't believe I have. And I don't believe He taught it, either. His ways are higher than our ways and also higher than the ways of the Mosaic law, which included an eye-for-an-eye justice. There are scriptures that speak of "vengeance" and related words, but when they do, they do not tell us that "vengeance is yours." It is uniquely God's, and I doubt He does it for the sake of revenge itself. As for following the example of the mortal Jesus Christ, we can do so without seeking revenge on the ungodly.

In fact, Christ explicitly taught us the opposite of revenge. He encouraged us to turn the other cheek, to go the extra mile, and to love our enemies, even though justice may *permit* (not require) retribution against such injustices. Justice is not robbed if retribution is not served. Justice can be served if another one of the purposes for punishment can be met: incapacitation, for example, which is another form of pure justice. Incapacitation, not retribution, may be the better answer when someone is beyond healing or rehabilitation. These kinds of criminals are incarcerated in jail or prison to incapacitate them from harming others. This deserved coercion is for the rare circumstances when we know someone is clearly beyond healing or recovery. In essence, justice can rightfully cause these criminals to follow the low standard of goodness that a lot of people praise as the greatest standard of goodness: do no harm.

Do No Harm Is a Low Standard of Morality: Let me elaborate on this for a moment. If "do no harm" is the best good that someone does, then their best good is at odds with the biblical standard found in James 4:17 and the one in modern revelation found in Doctrine and Covenants 59:26–29.

Christ teaches through the Epistle of James in the New Testament that "to him that knoweth to do good, and doeth it not, to him it is sin" (4:17). Clearly, then, simply not doing evil or not doing any harm is not good enough for Christ. To follow Christ, we must do all the good that we know to do.

But *know* is such a strong word, as we've previously discussed. So, is not *knowing* the good a suitable excuse for not doing good? That sounds like a good lawyerly loophole. The answer is no because Christ also teaches through modern revelation in the Doctrine and Covenants by a series of verses in section 58 that "it is not meet that I should command in all things; for he that is compelled in all things, the same is a slothful and not a wise servant" (v. 26). Without being told exactly what good to do, we must figure it ourselves.[3] Recall also

Professor Jaeger's comment that we don't have to know a person is in their true hour of need before we react.

Be Anxiously Engaged in Good and Seek Good Causes: Christ continues, "Verily I say, men should be anxiously engaged in a good cause, and do many things of their own free will, and bring to pass much righteousness" (v. 27). He explains, "For the power is in them, wherein they are agents unto themselves" (v. 28). As I understand these verses, we should be looking for opportunities to do good and to do it eagerly. He promises, "And inasmuch as men do good they shall in nowise lose their reward" (v. 28). This is an interesting promise because it implies that we have already been granted the reward; Christ's grace has already given it to us. The only way to lose the reward is through our own sin, or spiritual laziness in simply "doing no harm."

One last thing—Christ also warns, "But he that doeth not anything until he is commanded, and receiveth a commandment with doubtful heart, and keepeth it with slothfulness, the same is damned" (v. 29). It's understandable to not be proactively searching for good with the right attitude since it's such a higher law to keep, but when there is an explicit commandment from the Lord to do something, then we had better keep that direction with at least the hope that it came from Him and be diligent in following it. Else we will be utterly stopped in our spiritual progression.

Doing more than merely "doing no harm" elaborates on being more like Christ. Not settling for the low standard helps us come closer to Christ in an appropriate relationship with God. We need to better follow Him as His disciples and Christians. How we treat criminals can indicate our level of commitment. Rehabilitating them and being anxiously engaged in the *good cause* of healing them from their spiritual sicknesses can lead to the end of their criminal activity. This is hard work. Understandably, refraining from the effort and letting nature take its course is easier: "it is by the wicked that the wicked are punished" (Mormon 4:5). It's easier to let the criminals further ruin themselves while we refrain from being responsible for any harm to them. But they need help. They need rescuing. They need a physician, not our indifference. They need an advocate, not a mute observer.

3. Christ's Reaction to the Adulterous Woman: Loving with Initial Presumption-of-Innocence Attitude and Encouragement to Improve

> And the scribes and Pharisees brought unto him a woman taken in adultery; and when they had set her in the midst,
>
> They say unto him, Master, this woman was taken in adultery, in the very act.
>
> Now Moses in the law commanded us, that such should be stoned: but what sayest thou?
>
> This they said, tempting him, that they might have to accuse him. But Jesus stooped down, and with his finger wrote on the ground, as though he heard them not.
>
> So when they continued asking him, he lifted up himself, and said unto them, He that is without sin among you, let him first cast a stone at her.
>
> And again he stooped down, and wrote on the ground.
>
> And they which heard it, being convicted by their own conscience, went out one by one, beginning at the eldest, even unto the last: and Jesus was left alone, and the woman standing in the midst.
>
> When Jesus had lifted up himself, and saw none but the woman, he said unto her, Woman, where are those thine accusers? hath no man condemned thee?
>
> She said, No man, Lord. And Jesus said unto her, Neither do I condemn thee: go, and sin no more. (John 8:3–11)

This event is significant. It shows that without witnesses to stand by their accusations, or without *conclusive proof* of wrongdoing, a person should not be condemned for the wrong. They should be presumed innocent.

Presumption of Innocence: In another way of saying it, this event demonstrates that proof beyond a reasonable doubt, or knowledge of wrongdoing, should likely be the standard of truth that must be met before a person should be treated as guilty. We can be convinced of this because the Lord basically followed this principle.

Here, that standard of beyond a reasonable doubt was not met; therefore, Christ did not condemn or penalize the allegedly adulterous woman, but treated her as if she was innocent—He followed the presumption of innocence standard.

Christ's examination of this woman is an example of how the standards of truth, as described in prior chapters, come into play when scrutinizing people. As Christ did, we should give people accused of wrongs the benefit of the doubt, especially when the evidence is only supported by witnesses who have retracted their accusations or who are unwilling to stand by their prior testimonies.

Encourage the Sinner to Improve: The description of what happened shows one more highly significant fact, though. As Deity, Christ actually knew that she had committed the crime of adultery. So, how did He treat this criminal? What did He do to this sinner? He treated her with compassion and gave her words of encouragement to improve.

He told her that He didn't "condemn" her. He told her that she could go on with her life and "sin *no more.*" This compassionate encouragement is a spiritual balm of healing. Truly, Christ was her physician, seeking to remedy her from her sins, not execute her with condemnation, blame, unfairly sharp lecture, penalties, punishment, or otherwise.

Some may argue that He just empowered her to commit the sin again since He gave her no punishment for it. As rational as that position may be, the Lord God Jesus Christ apparently does not strictly follow that philosophy. He seems to follow a course of optimistic hope in the individual to willfully change her ways from the soft and gentle encouragement He gave her.

Let's go back to the discussion about the presumption of innocence Christ gave the adulterous woman. After seeing what Christ did here, can you, as a sincere follower of Christ, truly scold and censure a criminal defense attorney for demanding that the high standard (innocent until proven guilty beyond a reasonable doubt) be upheld, even though the client is probably a fully guilty criminal? Is the criminal defense attorney's role truly much different than the role Christ demonstrated here?

4. Christ's Association with Zacchaeus: Not Merely Association with a Sinner, but Loving Association with a Purpose to Save

> And Jesus entered and passed through Jericho.
>
> And, behold, there was a man named Zacchaeus, which was the chief among the publicans, and he was rich.
>
> And he sought to see Jesus who he was; and could not for the press, because he was little of stature.
>
> And he ran before, and climbed up into a sycamore tree to see him: for he was to pass that way.
>
> And when Jesus came to the place, he looked up, and saw him, and said unto him, Zacchaeus, make haste, and come down; for to day I must abide at thy house.
>
> And he made haste, and came down, and received him joyfully.
>
> And when they saw it, they all murmured, saying, That he was gone to be guest with a man that is a sinner.
>
> And Zacchaeus stood, and said unto the Lord; Behold, Lord, the half of my goods I give to the poor; and if I have taken any thing from any man by false accusation, I restore him fourfold.
>
> And Jesus said unto him, This day is salvation come to this house, forsomuch as he also is a son of Abraham.
>
> For the Son of man is come to seek and to save that which was lost. (Luke 19:1–10).

From this account, we see that Christ chose to associate with a known sinner. When the crowd saw it, "they all murmured, saying, That he was gone to be guest with . . . a sinner." Christ's purpose for associating with the sinner was not simply to be with him, but "to seek and to save that which was lost." Similarly, if we are to follow Christ and associate with sinners or criminals, then our purpose must include the intent to seek and to save someone who's lost.

Besides personal friends, work associates, and the family of a criminal, who else associates more with criminals than criminal defense attorneys? Who spends quality time with them like Christ did—time that is meant to "save that which was lost," to save them from pure retribution and give them the best chance at receiving rehabilitative help?

SUMMARIZING THE MANNERS IN WHICH CHRIST LOVES CRIMINALS

To summarize the manners in which Christ actively dealt with criminals in the last four examples, the list is as follows:

1. Loving patience, kindness, and forgiveness
2. Loving inquiries, healing, and compassion
3. Loving with initial presumption-of-innocence treatment and then encouragement to improve
4. Loving association among sinners with the purpose to save

CLEARING UP MISUNDERSTANDINGS

Maybe it would help to clear up a common mistaken understanding. I think many people believe that defense attorneys regularly get completely guilty criminals totally out of the justice system without the criminals facing any sort of consequence for their alleged actions. This isn't accurate.

It's uncommon for a defense attorney to make it possible for a guilty client to entirely escape justice through an outright dismissal of the case—our system doesn't allow it except for certain violations of the law by police (as discussed in chapter 4). At that point, the dismissal is *mandatory* by law. But these violations by law enforcement are not frequent; hence, the mandatory dismissals aren't either. Outside of the mandatory dismissals, the prosecutor would have to ignore legitimate evidence to the contrary (which evidence may or may not be accurate, but which would have to be examined at a trial to know one way or the other) and simply decide to dismiss the case outright in order for guilty clients to get off totally free. This just doesn't happen unless some form of corruption is taking place within the government or between the two lawyers. If this kind of corruption happens, it can't be often. I've never seen it.

It's also important to know that prosecutors will deliberately file charges against people that they know they can't prove are guilty and just hope that through the process, the defendant will fold and simply decide to plead guilty to avoid the risk of a more serious punishment for something he didn't do. It's unfair, and innocent people suffer from this.

PROSECUTION'S SLOPPY PROSECUTIONS

I once had a case where my client was charged with the serious second-degree felonies of theft and theft of a vehicle, both allegedly worth thousands of dollars.

My client had been living with his mother. A nephew had parked a broken down truck in the yard and was supposed to have been paying a rental fee to my client's mother. Years had gone by with no rent. At some point, the mother told my client that he could take the truck and sell it for money because she was owed so much by the nephew. He sincerely believed her and did. He received a couple hundred dollars for it, which is about what it was worth. He also sold the used generator the nephew had left in the garage and got about the same amount of money.

When the nephew found out, he was enraged. He filed charges against my client (not the mother). The prosecutors wanted my client to plead guilty to stealing thousands of dollars worth of property (even though he arranged for the return of the truck after learning of the mistake) and offered him two third degree felonies instead. But he never intended to steal or exercise unauthorized control over the property—he believed he had rightful permission to do what he did. He committed no crime, not even a misdemeanor. There can be no crime if there is no guilty mind. He had no guilty mind when he committed the acts of exercising unauthorized control over property that wasn't his.

My client also refused to make a plea bargain on the basis that the truck and generator together weren't even worth a thousand dollars. The plea bargain would have reduced the serious felony charges to misdemeanors had the prosecutors properly valued the property in the first place.

As soon as I told the judge that my client was demanding a preliminary hearing on the matter (a mini-trial to see if there's even enough evidence to go to trial over the accusations), the prosecutors immediately piped up and said they were withdrawing the charges against my client "so they could file more charges." The judge showed surprise that my client was getting such a good deal. We never had the preliminary hearing that was scheduled for that day. And to this day, the prosecutors have never filed any new charges.

In a noticeable amount of times, the prosecution and their charges are full of hot air. But that hot air can severely burn innocent people. It cost my client a lot of time, a fair amount of money in legal fees, and considerable stress to fight a case that should never have been filed in the first place. The prosecution had all the facts, and the facts clearly indicated that what my client did was a mistake, if anything—he did not deliberately intend to exercise unauthorized control over anyone's property. He had what he believed to be authorization from someone he believed had authority.

But because people are frequently arrested on trumped up charges and then have to fight those false charges or, at least, charges that are more serious than they should be, it is a very good day for a defense attorney to only get rehabilitative punishments for his client (instead of just reduced charges), who either already pled guilty or was found guilty; it is an even better day when a defense attorney gets a plea bargain that allows dismissal of the case after successful completion of a probationary-type period and conditions (the bargain is commonly referred to as a "plea in abeyance"); and it's almost his greatest day when he gets the very rare "diversion agreement" that dismisses the case immediately with minimal conditions and diverts prosecution for a later time—until and if the client violates the law during a probationary-type period in which the right to double jeopardy has been waived. These are all potential consequences a guilty person will most likely face.

You have to realize, though, that these resolutions are oftentimes what justice requires. There is no leniency involved because the original charges were already unfairly severe. Prosecutors or law enforcement will try to inflate the charges so that the plea bargain process, which reduces the charges, will result in roughly what they believe a defendant is actually guilty of. It's inappropriate and it happens too much—like the time when police initially cited my client for terrorism under the Patriot Act. He had filled a water bottle with liquid nitrogen at his job in the mall to see what would happen and then it exploded in an access hall that wasn't open to the public. As recorded by the court, the prosecution ended up charging it as a second-degree felony "incendiary device," which is an explosive capable of burning with an intense heat (under common usage of the term), punishable by up to fifteen years in prison and a fine close to twenty thousand dollars.

MORE OF CHRIST'S LOVING MANNERS

Visiting Prisoners and Using Wealth to Liberate the Captives: Before the prior theft example, we examined four significant examples from Christ's mortal life that showed the ways He loved others. I believe, however, there would have been many more examples of loving actions He did if we had a more complete record of our Savior's time on earth. I believe we would see instances when He visited criminals in prison (something criminal defense attorneys do as a part of their job). The reason I believe He would have done so is that He taught us to do so. Consider the following scriptures.

The words of Christ contained in the Book of Mormon explain that "before ye seek for riches, seek ye for the kingdom of God. And after ye have obtained a hope in Christ ye shall obtain riches, if ye seek them; and ye will seek them for the intent to . . . liberate the captive" (Jacob 2:18–19). Why would we use our wealth to liberate the captive? There's a very good reason: innocent people get imprisoned. The law school I attended, California Western School of Law, for example, had developed an "Innocence Program," which sought to re-examine the cases of people who were wrongfully imprisoned and ultimately release them back into society. That process is not a cheap process, but it yielded results—our school successfully exonerated a number of innocent people that had been wrongfully found guilty of crimes.

Christ taught this same doctrine, or different variations of a similar doctrine, in the scriptures:

> Matthew 25:34, 40—Then shall the King say unto them on his right hand, Come, ye blessed of my Father, inherit the kingdom prepared for you from the foundation of the world: . . . I was in prison, and ye came unto me. Then shall the righteous answer him, saying, Lord, when saw we thee . . . in prison, and came unto thee? And the King shall answer and say unto them, Verily I say unto you, Inasmuch as ye have done it unto one of the least of these my brethren, ye have done it unto me.

> Isaiah 58:6—Is not this the fast that I have chosen? to loose the bands of wickedness?

> Doctrine and Covenants 128:22—Brethren, shall we not go on in so great a cause? . . . King Immanuel . . . hath ordained, before the world was, that which would enable us to redeem them out of their prison; for the prisoners shall go free.
>
> Isaiah 49:6, 8–10—I will also give thee for a light to the Gentiles . . . and I will preserve thee, and give thee for a covenant of the people . . . to cause to inherit the desolate heritages; That thou mayest say to the prisoners, Go forth; to them that are in darkness, Shew yourselves . . . for he that hath mercy on them shall lead them.
>
> Isaiah 42:6–7—I the Lord have called thee in righteousness, and will . . . give thee . . . for a light of the Gentiles . . . to bring out the prisoners from the prison, and them that sit in darkness out of the prison house.

As I understand these verses, the Lord God Jesus Christ wants us to visit those in prison, loose the restrictive bands that wickedness wraps criminals in, and enable those spiritually incapacitated to become free souls through the light and mercy of the gospel and the ability of the Atonement to change a person's nature.

The Lord wants us to exercise the same mercy that He has shown in the past. One of these past examples comes from scripture out of ancient America: "And thus did the Spirit of the Lord work upon them, for they were the very vilest of sinners. And the Lord saw fit in his infinite mercy to spare them; nevertheless they suffered much anguish of soul because of their iniquities, suffering much and fearing that they should be cast off forever" (Mosiah 28:4). Even the "very vilest" of criminals who wish to be spared can be extended mercy after a period of proper punishment and suffering. Criminal defense attorneys understand this principle well because they regularly seek a rehabilitative punishment rather than a merely retributive punishment. And it is true. The fact is that some of the vilest criminals do need good solid punishment. But the hope for rehabilitation should never be extinguished. Neither should the effort to extend it.

Joy Over the Rehabilitated: God's reaction to the rehabilitated criminal is worth noting, as Christ plainly taught to the Pharisees who muttered among themselves and undervalued the worth of a reformed sinner when they saw Jesus associating and having meals with sinners:

> Then drew near unto him all the . . . sinners for to hear him. And the Pharisees and scribes murmured, saying, This man receiveth sinners, and eateth with them . . . . [Christ responded,] I say unto you, that likewise joy shall be in heaven over one sinner that repenteth, more than over ninety and nine just persons, which need no repentance. . . . I say unto you, there is joy in the presence of the angels of God over one sinner that repenteth. (Luke 15:1–2, 7, 10).

Consistent with this instruction that there will be divine joy in the rehabilitated criminal or sinner, Christ also taught about the sinner who would be raised up to a higher level of progression than the religious one who exalts himself above the "scum of the earth":

> The Pharisee stood and prayed thus with himself, God, I thank thee, that I am not as other men are, extortioners, unjust, adulterers, or even as this publican. . . . And the publican . . . smote upon his breast, saying, God be merciful to me a sinner. [Christ then explained] I tell you, this man went down to his house justified rather than the other: for every one that exalteth himself shall be abased; and he that humbleth himself shall be exalted. (Luke 18:11, 13–14).

The sinner or criminal is in a unique position for humility and growth. Once they humbly rehabilitate themselves, former criminals will be raised up or exalted above even the religiously pious who are prideful. Knowing this, a criminal defense attorney can reasonably maintain high hopes for even his guilty clients—hopes that they will want to do what it takes to improve and be changed for the better.

An example from Christ's life of a time when He presumably dealt with a serious transgressor, or someone who needed to be treated in much the same way as a transgressor, demonstrates the compassion, mercy, and proactive steps we should take toward healing the spiritually diseased.

> And when he was come out of the ship, immediately there met him out of the tombs a man with an unclean spirit,

Who had his dwelling among the tombs; and no man could bind him, no, not with chains:

Because that he had been often bound with fetters and chains, and the chains had been plucked asunder by him, and the fetters broken in pieces: neither could any man tame him.

And always, night and day, he was in the mountains, and in the tombs, crying, and cutting himself with stones.

But when he saw Jesus afar off, he ran and worshipped him,

And cried with a loud voice, and said, What have I to do with thee, Jesus, thou Son of the most high God? I adjure thee by God, that thou torment me not.

For he said unto him, Come out of the man, thou unclean spirit.

And he asked him, What is thy name? And he answered, saying, My name is Legion: for we are many.

And he besought him much that he would not send them away out of the country.

Now there was there nigh unto the mountains a great herd of swine feeding.

And all the devils besought him, saying, Send us into the swine, that we may enter into them.

And forthwith Jesus gave them leave. And the unclean spirits went out, and entered into the swine: and the herd ran violently down a steep place into the sea, (they were about two thousand;) and were choked in the sea.

And they that fed the swine fled, and told it in the city, and in the country. And they went out to see what it was that was done.

And they come to Jesus, and see him that was possessed with the devil, and had the legion, sitting, and clothed, and in his right mind: and they were afraid.

And they that saw it told them how it befell to him that was possessed with the devil, and also concerning the swine.

And they began to pray him to depart out of their coasts.

And when he was come into the ship, he that had been possessed with the devil prayed him that he might be with him.

Howbeit Jesus suffered him not, but saith unto him, Go home to thy friends, and tell them how great things the Lord hath done for thee, and hath had compassion on thee.

And he departed, and began to publish in Decapolis how great things Jesus had done for him: and all men did marvel. (Mark 5:2–20).

Here Christ helps a person who had presumably done such wrong that people tried to incapacitate him—wrong because he intended it or wrong because he was mentally ill. They tried to bind him, even with chains. Because of his connection to the power of evil, however, he had great strength and was able to escape from incapacitation, which "escape" is a crime in and of itself when the restriction was imposed as a result of criminal misconduct.

Notice how Christ treated this possible criminal (though some can contend he was not a criminal because the text never identified him as such, but the people treated him the same as a criminal in need of imprisonment). Christ immediately took the first steps of rehabilitating him by commanding the evil spirit to come out of him. When multiple devils spoke through the possible criminal, Christ diagnosed this man's problem further. He asked questions, much like a physician would to explore the nature of a sickness. This process ultimately produced what Christ had first commanded—the spirits leaving the criminal, but this time of their own volition. They *asked* Christ to cast them out of the man, which is what Christ did.

As the record describes, the possible criminal was clearly reformed. Under the law of justice, however, even a reformed criminal would usually have to answer for his untried crimes. This man could very well have still been guilty of escaping incarceration (if it was imposed upon him as a punishment, rather than for his own protection, as is the case for some people plagued with mental disorders. The only reason I persist in calling him a possible criminal is that he had a multitude of evil spirits possessing him—usually it takes proactive misconduct to draw in an evil spirit). He had never been tried for it (as far as we know).

Assuming that the man was guilty of escape, if Christ were being just according to mankind's law, then He would have required this man to go to the authorities and present himself to deal at least with the crime of escape. If our assumption is accurate, then we can learn that the Lord God follows a different way than mankind's justice. Christ, apparently, would want a changed man, not a punished man (arguably, possession by multiple devils that cause him to cry and cut himself in mountain tombs on a regular basis is punishment enough). Christ would have wanted others to see how a criminal had been reformed. He may have replaced strict legal justice with compassion and encouraged the man to tell his friends that the Lord had rehabilitated him. In this sense, He would have taken on a role similar to that of a criminal defense attorney instead of an executioner. These conclusions, though, are still subject to the man being a criminal. He may not have been; therefore, we cannot have a high degree of certainty in these particular deductions.

One of my clients, Jerry, ended up having to serve some jail time for white collar crime. Consider his story and you might see some rough parallels with the possessed man that Christ healed, including how the possessed man may have not been a criminal. Let me explain why Jerry doesn't necessarily fit the status of criminal but appears more as a victim of evil, just like the possessed man may have been.

Some investors had proposed a way for Jerry to make money. He tried it. It was initially bringing in some great returns for him. A couple of his friends asked him about how he was so successful. He eagerly told them of the investing opportunities he was doing. They also wanted to join in. In an effort to share his successes and wealth, Jerry helped them join, but shortly thereafter, the investment scheme turned out to be a scam.

Because Jerry failed to do his legally mandated "due diligence" on who the scamming investors actually were, which would have easily uncovered their fraudulent pasts, *and* because he also helped others eventually become scammed as a result of his own criminal negligence, he was guilty of white collar crime (even though he only had good intentions in trying to help his friends). It may not sound too criminal. And you're right. Typically, there must always be a guilty mind. Here, though, there was no guilty mind, only neglect. Jerry burned himself because of it. But the Utah legislature has deemed this kind of a mistake a crime because of the serious financial repercussions that can happen—you can get yourself *and* others into serious financial problems.

The "joy in heaven" part of the story, though, came from his experiences in jail. By the time he was released, he had started a Book of Mormon study group consisting of about twelve inmates. Even more amazing was that two of the participants had made commitments to get baptized into the Church by the time Jerry was finished with his thirty days in jail.

Jerry behaved like a reformed criminal who "began to publish in [jail] how great things Jesus had done for him: and all men did marvel" (Mark 5:20), like the reformed Legion who was originally possessed of devils. This "criminal," Jerry, demonstrates the reality that sometimes good people make bad mistakes. But just because they make bad mistakes does not mean they can't be reformed and do a lot of good in helping others be reformed in the process.

Christ Died for the Ungodly: All of the examples of Christ dealing with criminals and sinners can be summed up in Paul's insightful explanation of Christ's life mission in Romans 5:6, "Christ died for the *ungodly*." Who are more ungodly than criminals? Not many. The most heinous sins are usually crimes. Christ's life and death were to heal sinners and criminals, not penalize and punish them for their wrongs. "God commendeth his love toward us, in that, *while we were yet sinners*, Christ died *for us*" (Romans 5:8).

Perhaps one of the reasons why the Lord God Jesus Christ can be so kind, compassionate, and merciful toward sinners and criminals instead of being harsh and sharp with them as justice may allow is from what we briefly considered earlier. Justice will be met without His own penalizing intervention—the wicked will bring it upon themselves: "it is *by the wicked* that the wicked are punished" (Mormon 4:5) and "them that walk after the flesh in the lust of uncleanness . . . shall utterly perish *in their own corruption*" (2 Peter 2:10, 12).

As individuals, therefore, in following the example of Christ, we do not need to feel it our personal duty to severely and harshly criticize criminals and sinners in our thoughts or actions. Justice will be served without our personal intervention—it will be served either by the wicked to each other, by governments, disciplinary councils, or by Divine Intervention, or a combination of any of them.

But we don't stop there. We don't simply allow sin and non-judicially created punishment to take place. Instead, we are to individually be proactive healers of the spiritually sick. That demands of us kindness in all our dealings with others. To be this type of a healer, we must follow Christ's modern instruction that when "ye love one another . . . cease to find fault one with another" (D&C 88:123–124). This also means that "thou shalt weep . . . more especially for those that have not hope of a glorious resurrection." D&C 42:45. That also requires us to do all that we can to positively motivate and encourage people to do the right. We find a similar scripture in Psalms 51:13:—"Restore unto me the joy of thy salvation. . . . Then will I teach transgressors thy ways; and sinners shall be converted unto thee."

We can lovingly point out how people can change their wrongful behaviors to help them do better and be spiritually healed, but we do not need to be harsh. As the Lord taught in our day, those who proclaim His word "among the congregations of the wicked" are not to do it in "haste, neither in wrath nor with strife" (D&C 60:14).

There is no need to speak to criminals and sinners with impatience, anger, or combativeness. Instead, Jesus teaches, "And again, verily I say unto you, those who desire in their hearts, in meekness, to warn sinners to repentance, let them be ordained unto this power" (D&C 63:57). The method of warning sinners or counseling criminals is doing so in *meekness*. This is easy to do when you remember that God commands, "I, the Lord, will forgive whom I will forgive, but *of you it is required to forgive all men*" (D&C 64:10).

If we genuinely view criminals and sinners as the "scum of the earth," then we are certainly failing in our duty as disciples of Christ to be healers and physicians and to forgive all people, regardless of their degree of moral worthiness.

No Need to Fight Crime: If we believe we need to take it upon ourselves to individually "fight crime," rather than *heal crime*, we are not devoted disciples of Christ. Fighting crime is to be left to higher powers, such as governments, disciplinary councils, or God. Healing criminals and sinners is to be practiced by every dedicated Christian disciple. And a criminal defense attorney is uniquely situated to heal criminals for at least a couple reasons: (1) the criminal clients can trust their attorney like trusting a physician—their attorney will zealously fight for their rights (which includes demanding that they be presumed innocent until and if proven guilty beyond a reasonable doubt, as the divinely inspired Constitution directs) just as a doctor will fight to restore their health by treating their diseases regardless of how the diseases were acquired; and (2) if the criminal defendant's case goes to a guilty case, and then to sentencing for the guilt, then the criminal can trust that their legal representative will strongly advocate for rehabilitative punishments, rather than for retribution, which, again, is seeking for healing, not execution. I can think of no other occupation besides my own that deals so directly with criminals and sinners and advocates for rehabilitating and healing them, rather than condemning and executing retribution on them.

Christ Is Our Advocate: As the final point in this chapter, we need to keep in mind that scripture explicitly says, "And if any man sin, we have an advocate with the Father, Jesus Christ the righteous" (1 John 2:1).

Another popular translation of the whole verse reads, "My dear children, I write this to you so that you will not sin. But if anybody does sin, we have one who speaks to the Father in our defense—Jesus Christ, the Righteous One" (1 John 2:1, New International Version). Another popular translation puts it this way: "My dear children, I am writing this to you so that you will not sin. But if anyone does sin, we have an advocate who pleads our case before the Father. He is Jesus Christ, the one who is truly righteous" (1 John 2:1, New Living Translation).

This scripture is the basis for the name I gave my own law office. Why? Because Christ advocates for and defends sinners, including criminals. If He pleads their cases, then that's what I want to do on the small scale that I'm able to do so. In advocating their cause, He is still considered "righteous" or "just" (Douay-Rheims Bible, 1 John 2:1); therefore, there is no unrighteousness or injustice inherent in criminal defense attorneys advocating for, defending, and pleading the cases of criminals and pushing for their best interests. Consider also Micah 7:9, which says, "I will bear the indignation of the Lord, because I have *sinned* against him, until *he plead my cause*, and execute judgment for me" (emphasis added).

Notes

1. See also Mark 2:15–17; Luke 5:29–32.
2. I say "knowledge" because the information is God's position. And

the knowledge is academic in nature unless you have an independent verification. If the information was simply a man's opinion recorded in a book, then it would not be revealed or even recorded "knowledge," but it would simply be make-believe, reason, or philosophy.

3. This is an example where independence in spirituality is appropriate—once we have followed all the express commandments of the Lord, or as we're doing so, He expects us to be growing spiritually from it to the point that we recognize opportunities for doing various good things that aren't already spelled out for us.

18

THE REAL-LIFE EXAMPLES: WHO THESE CRIMINALS REALLY ARE

I OPENED THIS BOOK WITH A DESCRIPTION OF THE NIGHT WHEN Rico Martinez shot the driver of the opposing gang. But what really happened that night? The driver was an eyewitness of who shot him—it was Rico. The driver had seen Rico many times before. He saw Rico that evening at the gas station. Rico had thrown gang signs at him. He knew Rico's face when he saw it again only four hours later and only inches away from his own while it was illuminated by the street lamps and reflections off the snow. It was clearly Rico. Right?

The foregoing information came from the preliminary hearing on the matter that happened before Rico had been shot in retaliation for what he supposedly did to the opposing gang member driver. Then, weeks after the prelim, came the gas station video. The gas station video showed what Rico looked like on that night and what the other vehicle occupant looked like.

The video showed that in the vehicle that Rico had been a passenger, another occupant sat in the front passenger side. He was wearing a black tee-shirt. What was Rico wearing? The victim had said Rico was wearing a black tee-shirt. Rico wasn't wearing a tee-shirt by itself. His apparel wasn't black, either. He had on a *white* tee-shirt over a navy-blue, *long-sleeved* sweat shirt.

Rico's chin showed no sign of facial hair, but the other occupant's had what appeared to be shaved hair on his chin—just as the victim driver had described his attacker. Other than a light mustache, Rico couldn't grow facial hair—he had been trying for months, and, as a result, he had a few short, straggly, stray hairs on his chin. Where he could grow a lot of hair out was on his head—the video showed he clearly had a *non*-closely shaved head. But the victim driver said Rico's hair was closely shaven. Did anyone match that description? Yes, the other individual with the black tee-shirt had a very closely shaven head. Another important fact was that Rico had a clear scar on his face, but the victim driver said there was none. With the close proximity, he could have seen it, especially if he was scanning Rico's face for fifteen seconds or more, as he claimed he did at the prelim, while driving many others late at night downhill at high speeds. Further, the name "Rico Martinez" was the only personal name the driver even knew out of all of the opposing gang members in Rico's gang. Did it matter to him who got punished so long as it was someone from the other gang?

After pointing these deficiencies and many others out to the prosecutor, he finally dismissed the case. He had the wrong person. It wasn't Rico. Rico clearly was not the shooter. This was a case of mistaken identity. The victim driver also recanted his testimony to the prosecutor on a later occasion, which added to why the prosecutor dismissed the case against Rico.

The reason I share this is to show how basically normal people, like the prosecutor and the hooded assailants, easily make judgments that end up being draconian in nature when they rely only on what's reasonable. Because of the initial eyewitness account in police reports, it was clearly reasonable for a person to *believe* that Rico was the shooter. The prosecutor firmly believed it. But this initial witness identification testimony had never been tried. It had never been cross-examined to see if there were flaws or if it was the result of mistaken identity. In important matters, a higher degree of certainty must be demanded. The witness account in this case had not been put through the "crucible of cross-examination"[1] in order to achieve a higher degree of certainty. It still only amounted to probable cause, preponderance of the evidence, or perhaps even as high as clear and convincing evidence—all of which are evidentiary standards that would find a lot of innocent people to be criminals because they rely too much on reason, rational conclusions, and intellectuality in making final decisions.

More significantly, there were the two hooded individuals who took the reasonable *belief* along with the law into their own hands. For them, they were satisfied by reason—reason that what an eyewitness claims he saw must be absolutely true knowledge. And this is where relying on reason in important matters can lead to cruel outcomes—they approached Rico, and after confirming that it was him, they did three things without any regard to the separation of powers doctrine: (1) acted as the judiciary and made a final judgment that he was the shooter based on the merely reasonable *belief* that the untried eyewitness testimony of the driver was accurate; (2) decided that they had the right to punish such wrongdoing like a legislature would grant; and (3) carried out that punishment as the executive branch would. So, they shot him. They blasted him twice with a shower of shotgun pellets, injuring his hip and thumb to the point he had to be hospitalized.

In the end, however, after additional and powerful evidence, we all discovered conclusively that Rico was not the shooter. He was innocent of attempted murder. And yet he suffered for it. Had the two hooded individuals waited for knowledge before condemning and trying to execute Rico, the cruel outcome never would have happened to him. Even assuming they had "knowledge" that Rico was an attempted murderer, if they had abided in Christlike compassion for the supposed criminal and allowed the government to render judgment and impose execution rather than react with their own personal retribution toward the criminal, then they would not have tried to maim him, disfigure him, and destroy his life. And if they had left execution to higher powers, it would have proved especially beneficial for Rico because, in the end, he would never have been unjustifiably harmed. Thus, either knowledge of the actual truth or Christlike compassion by the hooded men would have prevented the harm that came to Rico.

Some of you may think, "Well, Rico wasn't innocent; he was a gang member." It does not matter. For disciples of Christ, Christlike compassion and using knowledge of facts in how we regard and treat others are fundamentally necessary no matter who is involved. Requiring a high standard of truth does not change. Being unconditionally compassionate to all others, even criminals, does not change.

While dealing with criminals, gang members, or anyone else, being compassionate will always demand a higher standard of truth than mere reason because of the real possibility that people should justly be treated more kindly. They should be treated according to what they actually committed or didn't commit. It may be of interest to note that Rico was not with those later that night when the shooting took place—he had been dropped off and was in another city with multiple friends who could corroborate his alibi.

LESSONS FROM THE RICO MARTINEZ CASE

Reason Alone Can Be Fatal: I use this example to help illustrate how acting on reasonable belief can be detrimental. Reasonable belief is what you have when you only have a limited quantity of evidence, or a low quality of evidence because it has not been tested. These kinds of evidence can only bring a limited amount of certainty about the truth. We need more exploration into the actual truth and a much higher resulting certainty when it comes to critically important matters. In relation to people matters, the deeper exploration is an act of love toward them because it helps prevent punishing the innocent.

It is certainly kind, compassionate, caring, and loving to defend people who are *wrongly* accused of crimes or sins. This preserves them from injustice. And injustice of any kind victimizes people and is a "threat to justice everywhere."[2]

Love Others by Demanding Knowledge of Guilt to Override the Presumption of Innocence: How we love others is the most critically important matter in life, with the exception of loving God. "Master, which is the great commandment in the law? Jesus said unto him, Thou shalt love the Lord thy God with all thy heart, and with all thy soul, and with all thy mind. This is the first and great commandment; And the second is like unto it, Thou shalt love thy neighbour as thyself. On these two commandments hang all the law and the prophets" (Matthew 22:36–40). Yet, loving others *is* loving God: "[W]hen ye are in the service of your fellow beings ye are only in the service of your God" (Mosiah 2:17) and "Inasmuch as ye have done it unto one of the least of these my brethren, ye have done it unto me" (Matthew 25:40). Complying with the two great commandments will make it so that "thy days may be prolonged" (which is a profound effect on one's mortal life) and make it so that "it may be well with thee, and that ye may increase mightily, as the Lord God of thy fathers hath promised thee" (which could even be understood to mean a mighty increase in *eternal* life, which profoundly affects one's life hereafter) (Deuteronomy 6:2–3).

Spirituality and religion—true religion particularly—teach us how to properly behave toward others, or how we should love them. Thus, spirituality and religion are critically important matters because they are capable of directly and profoundly affecting one's mortal life, and the mortal lives of others, and one's life in the hereafter for eternity. Accordingly, this means that for spiritual and religious matters, we must demand that we use higher standards of truth when choosing which spirituality and which religion to follow.

Unfortunately, too many people settle for relying only on what's reasonable in their spiritual or religious journeys. The ultimate outcome of such spiritual resignation cannot produce the best good and cannot totally avoid mistakes that have significantly harmful impacts on themselves and others. That same resignation carries over into their lives as jury members, and they sincerely think that it's satisfactory to say, "It's reasonable to believe that the defendant attempted to murder the driver—it just makes sense," and then apply a lifelong punishment as retribution for something that actually didn't happen. It's horribly unjust and terribly un-Christlike.

We must seek and receive knowledge, actual knowledge, either from a Divine Source or knowledge from evidence, rather than reason, on certain truths to avoid these injustices and un-Christlike outcomes. And then, if we gain knowledge that a person is guilty, we act compassionately with an eye toward healing his or her spiritual sickness instead of getting revenge for the willful misconduct. But we always must remember that if we are uncertain about a person's culpability, then we are to presume and treat that person as a child of God who is innocent of what he or she is accused of. And in the law, what a person is accused of is all that matters—he or she is not to receive punishment for *any other reason*.

Not Presuming Innocence Leads to Paranoia And Restrained Kindness: Without the presumption of innocence permanently guiding our judgments of others during the times when we lack contrary knowledge, we start out with the presumption that everyone is evil, or at least not innocent. We will then inevitably see a lot of innocent people as sinners and perceive more criminals in the world than there actually are. With the false belief that we are surrounded by more criminals than there actually are, we could easily become paranoid and perceive threats to ourselves and our loved ones that are unreal. Feeling threatened, we will likely treat others with *restrained* kindness in order to protect ourselves and our loved ones. Constrained kindness creates a breeding ground for pessimism and hate toward others. It's not what Christ wishes for us.

The Presumption of Innocence Leads to Christlike Behavior: But if we discard our complete reliance on rationality or intellectualism alone and insist on more knowledge of the truth before we determine a person's guiltiness, then we see there actually are fewer criminals and sinners. We will, therefore, feel less threatened and be able to respond toward others with unrestrained kindness, compassion, understanding, care, healing, and love. Those kinds of responses are fully Christlike. Those kinds of responses are how sincere followers of Christ act toward every enemy, sinner, and criminal. They do so even in meting out necessary punishments, or in defending one's self and others, and in reacting "betimes with sharpness" (D&C 121:43), but afterwards showing an increase in love.

The Virtues of Criminal Defense: It is also unconditionally compassionate to protect even the enemy, sinner, and criminal from unfair victimization by the legal system. Being a criminal defense attorney is an appropriate job for a sincere disciple of Christ because of the constant opportunities to protect people who are vulnerable to unjust treatment by the well-intentioned. The job allows you to extend love to those who especially need it because they may be spiritually sick and would not otherwise receive it; there may be too many people in their lives who make harsh judgments of them by relying solely on reason and intellectuality in such important matters. It is an honorable job for the sincere follower of the Lord God Jesus Christ because of the opportunities to heal and save that which is lost.

IN SUMMARY

Reason is frequently wrong in critically important matters and, as a result of heeding it, would condemn a person to criminal penalties: an unjustified loss of liberty, loss of financial means, loss of freedom from unnecessary mental institutions, or loss of other cherished rights. A disciple of Christ, therefore, must not use merely reason in his interpersonal dealings, especially when those decisions are in regard to accusations.

By seeking for and waiting patiently to obtain knowledge of the truth before making any condemnation, a disciple of Christ is charitable, compassionate, kind, humble, caring, merciful, and a peacemaker—all characteristics a defense attorney should have. And then if that knowledge comes, a disciple is not condemning, but still considerate and careful not to victimize even the "scum of the earth." He extends mercy or leniency to them in an effort to reform them, to heal them from their criminal sickness, and to encourage them in the process of becoming better individuals.

As a result of these Christlike responses to criminals, we will "be able to decrease the number of victims that result from the deviant behaviors" (see chapter 2) by eliminating the source of the deviant behaviors. That source is the criminal. We eliminate the criminal by converting him. We don't eliminate the criminal through discouraging criminal conduct. The conversion ultimately happens by Christ and His power to divinely reform individuals through His Atonement. That power to change can also come through rehabilitation programs designed to help the guilty overcome their challenges and become law-abiding citizens. And it is my testimony that Christ will certainly aid us in those outreaches, especially as we petition the Lord for His help.

Notes

1. *Crawford v. Washington*, 541 US 36, 61 (2004): "[The Sixth Amendment] commands, not that evidence be reliable, but that reliability be assessed in a particular manner: by testing in the crucible of

cross-examination. The clause thus reflects a judgment, not only about the desirability of reliable evidence (a point on which there could be little dissent), but about how reliability can best be determined." (Emphasis added)

2. Martin Luther King Jr., "Classic Quotes," The Quotations Page, http://www.quotationspage.com/quote/24974.html.

19

PROCESS OF ELIMINATION AND TESTIMONY

This book has discussed the idea that spirituality in the broad sense deals with how we interact with others. In order to avoid harmful interactions with criminals, and to promote the best way possible to heal them, we must ask ourselves what is the true, most ideal form of spirituality—the one that produces the most good toward others if followed? Or, in other words, the one that is Divinely approved?

We can't settle for man-made spirituality because it ends up lacking, which will eventually harm others and fail to lift them to their best potential. Not only must we ask what spirituality is objectively correct, but we also must fervently seek the actual answer from the Source of all truth. Then we wait patiently for at least some knowledge on the matter coming from that Source alone.

We must also ask ourselves, "Once I find the true and proper spirituality, is there a religion approved of by Diety that incorporates it?" Without knowledge on this matter, people are left to use reason and intellectualism to make educated guesses and fill in the gaps. And, as discussed throughout the book, in critically important matters, reason and intellectualism too frequently make mistakes. The mistakes they make can be of the most harmful kind to the individual and to others.

As I stated in the beginning, this book is essentially my testimony—my legal and spiritual testimony. Since I've already detailed my legal and scriptural testimony, let me specifically add my personal testimony about what I know concerning spiritual and religious truths. From my own sacred, personal experiences, I know which spirituality and religion are true. This knowledge is available for everyone to also gain for themselves as eyewitnesses to the truth or through a gift to believe. But, until then, if you haven't gained it, let me share with you how my testimony has developed to provide you with a basis for belief, the lowest degree of certainty from the Spiritual Truth Scrutiny tests (see chapters 9 to 11).

Some of those experiences have even given me a perfect or absolute knowledge of the truth. The Gospel of Jesus Christ, when followed as He directs, is the true form of spirituality. The Church of Jesus Christ of Latter-day Saints incorporates that spirituality and is Christ's true religion. It is the one Christ founded anciently, restored modernly, and totally approves of currently. It is the one He personally would attend if He were on earth and walking among us. It's the one He would have all of us attend and actively support for the benefit of all people on earth and in the spirit world.

There are five foundational testimony or eyewitness experiences that I gained early on, which have brought this knowledge to me from the Divine Source of All Truth. These five experiences each brought me the following pieces of knowledge. They are listed in the order I received them together with what I learned at the time I experienced them and include the degree of certainty I judge that I have in these areas:

1. GOD: A God or Supreme Being exists that is beyond the ability of the natural body and mind to create or replicate (*absolute knowledge*).

2. REVELATION: This God not only exists, but He is also highly involved with us—He cares about us and communicates with us about matters that are presently important to us (*knowledge*).

3. CHRIST: Jesus Christ lives as an actual Being of tremendous love and can be trusted without reservation as a fully capable Protector from evil as I rely on Him (*knowledge*).

4. SCRIPTURE: The Book of Mormon is the word of this same Jesus Christ—it contains His words and it is His book of scripture for all of us (along with the Bible, which I know is also His book through knowledge by extension) (*knowledge*).

5. RELIGION: The Church of Jesus Christ of Latter-day Saints is uniquely true as Christ's own, organized religion (*absolute knowledge*).

I've included a brief description of these truths in the column headings of the chart below and a number in parenthesis next to it. Each column lists twenty different and, hopefully, fairly representative faiths from around the world. I picked these faiths because they are based on my personal experiences that I've had with each one of them, all of which have been very positive, uplifting, and have provided me with "virtue" (see Article of Faith 13). The number in parenthesis next to the heading statement shows how many of the twenty faiths are narrowed down by the specific witness of truth I received for myself. The narrowing is based only on a general understanding of the faith and does not represent what every believer of the particular faith may feel about it.

For example, certain kinds of Taoism include a belief in a pantheon of gods that may care about us while other forms of Taoism are more philosophical and do not focus on deities. This chart treats Taoism as the kind that is more philosophical than spiritual or religious.

Also, under the column heading, "Jesus Christ is Protector," Islam is *not* excluded. This may seem contrary to many people's understandings of Muslim theology, but according to my Muslim professor I had in Jerusalem while I did a study abroad there, Islam teaches that the prophet Jesus sits at the right hand of Allah and he will one day descend to the earth and confirm Allah's true teachings. In that sense, I do not treat Islam as eliminating Jesus as a "protector." He is essentially a protector of truth. And truth, in turn, can protect us.

As each foundational testimony of truth came, I would have been able to narrow down the world faiths if I were as familiar with their general teachings as I am now. I gained this familiarity by personal study of their own claims—not the claims that others make about their claims. I did not rely on any anti-their-particular-faith material because all I need is the Spirit to guide me as I study what they themselves describe their religion as. Anti-any-religion material usually carries with it unfair prejudice, inaccurate descriptions that frequently come from unreliable, offended people, and often have a Satanic influence—or at least an influence that is not of Christ. It's always best to go to the source, the religion itself, if you want to learn about it. Then petition God for a proper understanding of what the truth of the religion or its teachings is.

I present this chart on pages 180–181 to help people in their spiritual journeys. The journey should end at the most ideal, absolutely true, and fully universal spirituality and religion. Then, at this point, they will come to know with certainty how to most appropriately behave in love toward and rightly consider the "accused," the guilty "criminal," the "enemy," and the "sinner." People should be able to appreciate the morality in defending the criminal and being an advocate for the criminal's best interests.

Foundational Testimony Experiences: Narrowing the Options

1. God exists (1)	2. God cares about us (7)	3. Jesus Christ is Protector (10)	4. Book of Mormon is true (16)	5. LDS Church is true (19)
~~Atheism~~	~~Atheism~~	~~Atheism~~	~~Atheism~~	~~Atheism~~
Agnosticism	~~Agnosticism~~	~~Agnosticism~~	~~Agnosticism~~	~~Agnosticism~~
Buddhism	~~Buddhism~~	~~Buddhism~~	~~Buddhism~~	~~Buddhism~~
Taoism	~~Taoism~~	~~Taoism~~	~~Taoism~~	~~Taoism~~
Confucianism	~~Confucianism~~	~~Confucianism~~	~~Confucianism~~	~~Confucianism~~
Shintoism	~~Shintoism~~	~~Shintoism~~	~~Shintoism~~	~~Shintoism~~
Jainism	~~Jainism~~	~~Jainism~~	~~Jainism~~	~~Jainism~~
Sikhism	Sikhism	~~Sikhism~~	~~Sikhism~~	~~Sikhism~~
Hinduism	Hinduism	~~Hinduism~~	~~Hinduism~~	~~Hinduism~~
Judaism	Judaism	~~Judaism~~	~~Judaism~~	~~Judaism~~

Islam	Islam	Islam	~~Islam~~	~~Islam~~
Catholicism	Catholicism	Catholicism	~~Catholicism~~	~~Catholicism~~
Protestantism	Protestantism	Protestantism	~~Protestantism~~	~~Protestantism~~
Non-denomenation-alism	Non-denomenation-alism	Non-denomenation-alism	~~Non-denomenation-alism~~	~~Non-denomenation-alism~~
Seventh-Day Adventists	Seventh-Day Adventists	Seventh-Day Adventists	~~Seventh-Day Adventists~~	~~Seventh-Day Adventists~~
Jehovah's Witnesses	Jehovah's Witnesses	Jehovah's Witnesses	~~Jehovah's Witnesses~~	~~Jehovah's Witnesses~~
Baha'i Faith	Baha'i Faith	Baha'i Faith	Baha'i Faith	~~Baha'i Faith~~
Apostolic United Brethren	Apostolic United Brethren	Apostolic United Brethren	Apostolic United Brethren	~~Apostolic United Brethren~~
Community of Christ	Community of Christ	Community of Christ	Community of Christ	~~Community of Christ~~
Mormonism	Mormonism	Mormonism	Mormonism	Mormonism

ABOUT THE AUTHOR

As an Eagle Scout and black belt in karate, Mr. Taylor C. Hartley, Esq. served a mission for The Church of Jesus Christ of Latter-day Saints in Seoul, South Korea, where he was also a Korean Sign Language elder. Once his mission was honorably completed, he earned his bachelor's degree in psychology in less than two academic years after studying at Ricks College, the BYU Jerusalem Center for Near Eastern Studies, and Brigham Young University. One of his favorite jobs during school was teaching missionaries at the Missionary Training Center in Provo, Utah.

Mr. Hartley pursued a Juris Doctor degree at California Western School of Law in San Diego where he had one of the best scholarships the school offers. Because of his grades in the first year of law school, he was selected to be a "large group tutor" for seventy incoming students and to be a notetaker for disabled and foreign students in many law school classes for the remaining two years of his studies. While in California, he gained work experiences in Family, Workers Compensation, Employment, Franchise, Contract, Construction, and Corporate law.

Shortly after finishing law school, he married his wife, Jamie, and moved home to Utah. With only self-study as preparation, Mr. Hartley took and passed the Utah Bar exam. While clerking for a local criminal defense firm that inspired his strong interest in criminal law, he and his wife formed a non-profit organization (The United Survivors with Epidermolysis Bullosa) to help people with a rare genetic skin disorder become more self reliant. He was hired as a judicial law clerk for the Fourth District Court of Utah and later taught Criminology (the study of crime and why people commit it) and two other courses as an instructor at Provo College. While working as an associate attorney at a family law firm, he formed his own criminal defense practice and joined the largest association of criminal defense lawyers in Utah (UACDL).

Because of his own practice's success, he left the firm and began working as a solo practitioner in criminal defense at his company, The Advocate Attorney, LLC. Over the years, he has found meaningful purpose in continuing to help people charged with criminal violations of the law and in aggressively protecting their constitutional rights. For him, work is more of a service than a business. He is also in the initial stages of preparing a pre-law academy that will help people decide whether they want to pursue a legal career and help interested individuals both succeed in law school and gain a greater capacity to serve their communities effectively as well-trained and ethical lawyers.

0 26575 57991 8